G. C. Grubb

Convenanted Blessings

Seven Bible Readings

G. C. Grubb

Convenanted Blessings
Seven Bible Readings

ISBN/EAN: 9783337095994

Printed in Europe, USA, Canada, Australia, Japan

Cover: Foto ©Lupo / pixelio.de

More available books at **www.hansebooks.com**

Covenanted Blessings

SEVEN BIBLE READINGS

GIVEN BY

REV. G. C. GRUBB, M.A.

"TO THE JEW FIRST, AND ALSO TO THE GENTILE."
Romans i. 16, ii. 9, 10.

London:
MARSHALL BROTHERS, KESWICK HOUSE,
PATERNOSTER ROW, E.C.
1893.

Editorial Note.

THE following chapters contain the substance of seven Bible Readings, given during January and February, 1893, at the Bethshan Hall, Drayton Park, N., and at the Paddington Baths, Queen's Road, W., by the REV. G. C. GRUBB, M.A.

"TO THE JEW FIRST, AND ALSO TO THE GENTILE."

MAY, 1893.

Contents.

1. THREE UNCONDITIONAL COVENANTS ... 9
2. THE SEED OF THE WOMAN 25
3. A PROPHET LIKE UNTO MOSES 43
4. AN ETERNAL PRIEST 61
5. THE KING OF GLORY 77
6. WHAT IS HIS SON'S NAME? ... 95
7. THE PASSOVER LAMB 113

R. W. SIMPSON.
PRINTER
RICHMOND, LONDON.

I.

Three Unconditional Covenants.

Although my house be not so with God ; yet He hath made with me an everlasting covenant, ordered in all things, and sure ;
2 Samuel xxiii. 5.

God is not a man, that He should lie ; neither the son of man, that He should repent : hath He said, and shall He not do it? or hath He spoken, and shall He not make it good ?
Numbers xxiii. 9.

He will ever be mindful of His covenant.
Psalm cxi. 5.

If we believe not, yet He abideth faithful : He cannot deny Himself.
2 Timothy ii. 13.

Covenanted Blessings.

Three Unconditional Covenants.

As a foundation for our study let us read Ps. lxxxix. 1-4:

"I will sing of the mercies of the LORD for ever: with my mouth will I make known Thy faithfulness to all generations. For I have said, Mercy shall be built up for ever: Thy faithfulness shalt Thou establish in the very heavens. I have made a covenant with My chosen, I have sworn unto David My servant, Thy seed will I establish for ever, and build up thy throne to all generations."

The only reason that God leaves us a little longer in the world is that we may show forth His faithfulness; and your life is of no good to God—whether you are Jews or Gentiles—unless each day you influence some one around you to trust more in God than when he rose in the morning. "With my mouth will I make known Thy faithfulness to all generations."

To-night I would say a little about the three pillars upon which the Old Testament is built; and I might also say the New Testament, for the New Testament is only a continuation of the Old. These pillars are the THREE UNCONDITIONAL COVENANTS of God. I say *unconditional*, for a covenant can be a covenant of grace, or a covenant of works. If I make a promise to you, 'I will do this thing for you,' that is an unconditional covenant—I bind myself to do it for you. But if I say: 'I will do that for you if you will do something for me,' that is a conditional promise.

The three unconditional covenants were made by God. One with Noah, concerning the world; the second with Abraham, concerning the land of Canaan; and the third with David, concerning his throne. And upon these three covenants all human history is based. I will prove that.

Turn with me to Gen. ix. 8-17: "And God spake unto Noah, and to his sons with him, saying, And I, behold, I establish My covenant with you, and with your seed after you; and with every living creature that is with you, of the fowl, of the cattle, and of every beast of the earth with you; from all that go out of the ark, to every beast of the earth: And I will establish My covenant with you; neither shall all flesh be cut off any more by the waters of a flood; neither shall there any more be a flood to destroy the earth. And God said, This is the token of the covenant which I make between Me and you, and every living creature that is with you, for perpetual generations: I do set My bow in the cloud, and it shall be for a token of a covenant between Me and the earth. And it shall come to pass, when I bring a cloud over the earth, that the bow shall be seen in the cloud: and I will remember My covenant, which is between Me and you, and every living creature of all flesh; and the waters shall no more become a flood to destroy all flesh. And the bow shall be in the cloud: and I will look upon it, that I may remember the everlasting covenant between God and every living creature of all flesh that is upon the earth. And God said unto Noah, This is the token of the covenant, which I have established between Me and all flesh that is upon the earth."

This covenant secures to us all the privileges of food and clothing, rain and sunshine, showers and fruitful seasons; for "while the earth remaineth, seed-time and harvest, and cold and heat, and summer and winter, and day and night, shall not cease." So when you get up to-morrow morning, remember the sun is shining because God made a covenant with Noah, and the darkness that is around us now rests upon the same word of promise. When you eat an apple, thank God because it is included in His covenant with Noah; and when you eat bread, remember that He said "seed-time and harvest shall not cease." How we should thank God for this: yet one of the great marks of the world to-day is that men are not thankful to God. And in Romans Paul speaks of this as one of the depths of sin into which the heathen had fallen: "Because that, when they knew God, they glorified Him not as God, neither were thankful." (Chap. i. 21.) Praise God for His covenant with Noah. Praise God for all temporal blessings. I beseech you do not take your breakfast in the morning, and your dinner, and afternoon tea, and supper as matters of course; but give God thanks for all: they are all the gifts of His grace.

"Every good gift and every perfect gift, is from above, and cometh down from the Father of lights, with Whom is no variableness, neither shadow of turning." (Jas. i. 17.) "He left not Himself without witness, in that He did good, and gave us rain from heaven, and fruitful seasons, filling our hearts with food and gladness." (Acts xiv. 17.)

The second unconditional covenant you will find in Gen. xv. 7-21, where God said unto Abram, "I am the LORD that brought thee out of Ur of the Chaldees, to give thee this land to inherit it. And he said, Lord God, whereby shall I know that I shall inherit it? . . . And He said unto him, Take Me an heifer of three years old, and a she-goat of three years old, and a ram of three years old, and a turtledove, and a young pigeon." Those were all clean animals that were used in sacrifice. "And he took unto him all these, and divided them in the midst, and laid each piece one against another: but the birds divided he not. And when the fowls came down upon the carcases, Abram drove them away. And when the sun was going down, a deep sleep fell upon Abram; and, lo, an horror of great darkness fell upon him. And He said unto Abram, Know of a surety that thy seed shall be a stranger in a land that is not theirs, and shall serve them; and they shall afflict them four hundred years: And also that nation, whom they shall serve, will I judge: and afterward shall they come out with great substance. And thou shalt go to thy fathers in peace; thou shalt be buried in a good old age. But in the fourth generation they shall come hither again: for the iniquity of the Amorites is not yet full. And it came to pass, that, when the sun went down, and it was dark, behold a smoking furnace, and a burning lamp that passed between those pieces. In the same day the LORD made a covenant with Abram, saying, Unto thy seed have I given this land, from the river of Egypt unto the great river, the river Euphrates: the Kenites, and the Kenizzites, and the Kadmonites, and the Hittites, and the Perizzites, and the Rephaims, and the Amorites, and the Canaanites, and the Girgashites, and the Jebusites."

The Jews are now practically out of the land of Canaan, and have been out for the last eighteen hundred years, and the ten tribes have been scattered much longer than that; yet the twelve tribes must be restored to Palestine, in order that God's Word may be fulfilled, for the Scripture cannot be broken.

Notice that the entrance into this covenant on Abram's side was by faith. In verse 5, of the same chapter we read that God "brought him forth abroad, and said, Look now toward heaven, and tell the stars, if thou be able to number them; and He said unto him, So shall thy seed be. And he believed in the LORD; and He counted it to him for righteousness. And He said unto him, I am the LORD that brought thee out of Ur of the Chaldees, to give thee this land to inherit it. And he said, Lord GOD, whereby shall I know that I shall inherit it?" So soon as Abram believed God that his seed would be as the stars of heaven, God said: "I will give thee the land of Canaan." So Abram received the land by faith, and the Holy Spirit's commentary on this is in Rom. iv. It will encourage our faith if we read this chapter: I have read it many times, and each time it has strengthened my faith.

"What shall we then say that Abraham our father, as pertaining to the flesh, hath found? For if Abraham were justified by works, he hath whereof to glory; but not before God. For what saith the Scripture? Abraham believed God, and it was counted unto him for righteousness. Now to him that worketh is the reward not reckoned of grace, but of debt. But to him that worketh not, but believeth on Him that justifieth the ungodly, his faith is counted for righteousness. Even as David also describeth the blessedness of the man, unto whom God imputeth righteousness without works, saying, Blessed are they whose iniquities are forgiven, and whose sins are covered. Blessed is the man to whom the LORD will not impute sin. Cometh this blessedness then upon the circumcision only, or upon the uncircumcision also? For we say that faith was reckoned to Abraham for righteousness. How was it then reckoned? When he was in circumcision, or in uncircumcision? Not in circumcision, but in uncircumcision. And he received the sign of circumcision, a seal of the righteousness of the faith which he had, yet being uncircumcised; that he might be the father of all them that believe, though they be not circumcised; that righteousness might be imputed unto them also: And the father of circumcision to them who are not of the circumcision only, but who also walk in the steps of that faith of our father Abraham, which he had being yet uncircumcised. For the promise, that he should be the heir of the world, was not to Abraham, or to his seed, through the law, but through the righteousness of faith. For if they which are of the law be heirs, faith is made void, and the promise made of none effect: Because the law worketh wrath: for where no law is, there is no transgression."

Of course there is not; for how can you transgress my law when I have given you no law? "Whosoever committeth sin transgresseth also the law: for sin is the transgression of the law." (1 John iii. 4.)

"Therefore it is of faith, that it might be by grace; to the end the promise might be sure to all the seed: Not to that only which is of the law, but to that also which is of the faith of Abraham, who is the father of us all, (As it is written, I have made thee a father of many nations)."

Notice the change of name from Abram, an exalted father, to Abraham, a father of many nations, in Gen. xvii. 5: and remember you can only be what God calls you. " Behold, what manner of love the Father hath bestowed upon us, that we should be called children of God: and such we are," is the R.V. of 1 John iii. 1.

Let us follow Abraham's faith, " Who against hope believed in hope, that he might become the father of many nations, according to that which was spoken, So shall thy seed be. And being not weak in faith, he considered not his own body now dead." To get the full force of this passage we must turn for a few verses to the Revised Version.

Some say, 'You must not look at difficulties and trials,' but real faith does look at them, and reckons that God is able to overcome them. "Without being weakened in faith he considered his own body now as good as dead (he being about a hundred years old), and the deadness of Sarah's womb : yea, looking unto the promise of God, he wavered not through unbelief, but waxed strong through faith, giving glory to God, and being fully persuaded that, what He had promised, He was able also to perform. And therefore it was imputed to him for righteousness. Now it was not written for his sake alone, that it was imputed to him : But for us also, to whom it shall be imputed, if we believe on Him that raised up Jesus our Lord from the dead ; Who was delivered for our offences, and was raised again for our justification."

But Abraham died without seeing the fulfilment of these unconditional promises. "These all died in faith, not having received the promises, but having seen them afar off, and were persuaded of them, and embraced them, and confessed that they were strangers and pilgrims on the earth." (Heb. xi. 13.) What a temptation to doubt that must have been to Abraham as he felt his strength withering ; knowing that in the promised land he had only a few feet of ground for a grave for Sarah, and that he had had to buy ! When the Sadducees attempted to entangle Christ in His talk about the resurrection, (Mark xii. 26, 27) He said : " Have ye not read in the book of Moses, how in the bush God spake unto him, saying, I am the God of Abraham, and the God of Isaac, and the God of Jacob? He is not the God of the dead, but the God of the living." Christ's argument is this : Abraham, Isaac, and Jacob are dead. God made several promises to them. Those promises were not fulfilled during their life-time, but God's Word cannot be broken; therefore God will raise up Abraham, Isaac, and Jacob from the dead, in order that He may fulfil His promises literally to them hereafter. The people saw the point at once, and after that it is said they were afraid to ask Him any more questions. So God's promises of grace are based upon the resurrection—upon the fact that God can call you back from the dead and fulfil His promises. We have a grand God to deal with: so let us trust Him through thick and thin, even when we do not see the way.

The third unconditional covenant is with David, concerning the throne, in 2 Sam. vii. 12-29:

"And when thy days be fulfilled, and thou shalt sleep with thy fathers, I will set up thy seed after thee, which shall proceed out of thy bowels, and I will establish his kingdom. He shall build a house for My name, and I will stablish the throne of his kingdom for ever. I will be his Father, and he shall be My son. If he commit iniquity, I will chasten him with the rod of men, and with the stripes of the children of men: But My mercy shall not depart away from him, as I took it from Saul, whom I put away before thee. And thine house and thy kingdom shall be established for ever before thee: thy throne shall be established for ever. According to all these words, and according to all this vision, so did Nathan speak unto David. Then went king David in, and sat before the LORD, and he said, Who am I, O Lord GOD? and what is my house, that Thou hast brought me hitherto? And this was yet a small thing in Thy sight, O Lord GOD; but Thou hast spoken also of Thy servant's house for a great while to come. And is this the manner of man, O Lord GOD? And what can David say more unto Thee? For Thou, Lord GOD, knowest Thy servant. For Thy word's sake, and according to Thine own heart, hast Thou done all these great things, to make Thy servant know them. Wherefore Thou art great, O LORD God: for there is none like Thee, neither is there any God beside Thee, according to all that we have heard with our ears. And what one nation in the earth is like Thy people, even like Israel, whom God went to redeem for a people to Himself, and to make Him a name, and to do for you great things and terrible, for Thy land, before Thy people, which Thou redeemedst to Thee from Egypt, from the nations and their gods?"

Have you been redeemed to God? Not to yourself, or to selfishness, or to social position in the world, but to God? That is the very thing that is said in the Epistle to Titus. He "gave Himself for us, that He might redeem us from all iniquity, and purify unto Himself a people for His own possession, zealous of good works." (Chap. ii. 14, R.V.)

"For Thou hast confirmed to Thyself Thy people Israel, to be a people unto Thee for ever; and Thou, LORD, art become their God. And now, O LORD God, the word that Thou hast spoken concerning Thy servant, and concerning his house, establish it for ever, and do as Thou hast said. And let Thy name be magnified for ever, saying, The Lord of hosts is the God over Israel: and let the house of Thy servant David be established before Thee. For Thou, O LORD of hosts, God of Israel, hast revealed to Thy servant, saying, I will build thee a house; therefore hath Thy servant found in his heart to pray this prayer unto Thee."

Whenever God gives you a promise from His Book turn it into prayer, for that is the way to appropriate it. Some say, 'I have all things in Christ, so I have nothing more to receive.' Do not misunderstand God's unconditional covenant. It is true that you are blessed with all spiritual blessings in Christ;

(Eph. i. 3) but by faith you must draw from this rich supply of grace. "Believe that ye receive them, and ye shall have them." "Let him ask in faith, nothing wavering. For he that wavereth is like a wave of the sea driven with the wind and tossed. For let not that man think that he shall receive anything of the Lord." (Mark xi. 24; James i. 6, 7.) Israel too must turn to God in supplication and in faith, before they can receive from Him the fulfilment of His "exceeding great and precious promises." (Zech. xii. 10; 2 Pet. i. 4.)

"And now, O Lord God, Thou art that God, and Thy words be true," (Hebrew, "truth") "and Thou hast promised this goodness unto Thy servant; therefore now let it please Thee to bless the house of Thy servant, that it may continue for ever before Thee: for Thou, O Lord God, hast spoken it: and with Thy blessing let the house of Thy servant be blessed for ever."

In the last words of David (2 Sam. xxiii. 5) we have a touching reference to this glorious covenant:

"Although my house be not so with God; yet He hath made with me an everlasting covenant, ordered in all things, and sure." Here, as in Rom. iv., the word "sure" is used; for everything in grace is sure. These covenants are sure, though all the politicians in the world might try to frustrate their fulfilment.

Now turn with me to a passage of Scripture which sums up all I have said, where the three unconditional covenants are mentioned together. Jer. xxxiii. 14-17; 19-26: "Behold, the days come saith the Lord, that I will perform that good thing which I have promised unto the house of Israel and to the house of Judah. In those days, and at that time, will I cause the Branch of righteousness to grow up unto David."

Nearly all Rabbinical writers, without exception,

apply this verse to the Messiah, and the following words prove that the Branch is a person: " And He shall execute judgment and righteousness in the land. In those days shall Judah be saved, and Jerusalem shall dwell safely: and this is the name wherewith she shall be called, The LORD our righteousness. For thus saith the LORD, David shall never want a man to sit upon the throne of the house of Israel ;"

And yet, according to outward appearance, David has wanted a man for over two thousand years; for the earthly kings of David's line ceased when the Jews were taken captive to Babylon. The only man who is known to be living at the present day of the lineage of David is the Lord Jesus Christ; for all the Jewish genealogies perished at the destruction of Jerusalem; so that no Jew now can be sure of his genealogy: and the latest genealogies we have to-day are those in the gospels of Matthew and Luke; the one traces the descent of Jesus back through Solomon to David, and the other through Nathan. The genealogy in Matthew is only traced back to Abraham. " The book of the genealogy of Jesus Christ, the son of David, the son of Abraham." But in Luke you will find Jesus as " the seed of the woman," and there it goes back to Adam. The Jews never reckoned the woman. Heli was the father of Mary, and, of course, the father-in-law of Joseph; but, as was usual with the Jews, Joseph is said to be the son of Heli. So the only genealogy left now is that of Jesus, who is alive, and David does not want a man to sit on his throne. The kingdom is in heaven, therefore the King is hidden. As it was in the days of Athaliah, so it is now. When Athaliah was in the land, the king was hidden in the temple. He is now hidden in the temple of God up there, but the time is coming quickly when His people's hearts are to turn to Him, and God will see Israel yet rejoice because their King is come: even Jesus, who was born King of the Jews. He offered Himself in the last week of his life as King to the Jews, and they rejected Him, and in that very week, four hundred and eighty-three years "from the going forth of the commandment to restore and to build Jerusalem," were fulfilled to the very day. (See Dan. ix. 25.) And on that day Jesus said: (Luke xix. 42-44) "If thou hadst known, even thou, at least in this thy day, the things which belong unto thy peace! But now they are hid from thine eyes. For the days shall come upon thee, that thine enemies shall cast a trench about thee, and compass thee round, and keep thee in on every side, and shall lay thee even with the ground, and thy children within thee; and they shall not leave in thee one stone upon another: because thou knewest not the time of thy visitation."

But the King is coming again, and we are the hidden members of His body in the meantime, for our "life is hid with Christ in God." (Col. iii. 3.) But soon the King shall be manifested in glory; so we need not be downcast, but bear ourselves with dignity, and make our boast in our God. As David said, "In God we boast all the day long, and praise Thy Name for ever." "My soul shall make her boast in the LORD: the humble shall hear thereof, and be glad." (Ps. xliv. 8, and xxxiv. 2.)

Let us read to the end of our chapter in Jeremiah. "And the word of the Lord came unto Jeremiah, saying, Thus saith the LORD, If ye can break My covenant of the day, and My covenant of the night, and that there should not be day and night in their season: Then may also My covenant be broken with David My servant, that he should not have a son to reign upon his throne; and with the Levites the priests, My ministers. As the host of heaven cannot be numbered, neither the sand of the sea measured:

so will I multiply the seed of David My servant, and the Levites that minister unto Me. Moreover the word of the Lord came to Jeremiah, saying, Considerest thou not what this people have spoken, saying, The two families which the Lord hath chosen, He hath even cast them off? thus they have despised My people, that they should be no more a nation before them."

Note here that God notices what we say about His Word. It is dangerous to speak lightly or unadvisedly about the Word of God.

Apparently God had cast them off. They were all in captivity; the ten tribes in Assyria, and Judah in Babylon; so people saw a great deal in favour of unbelief. Facts seemed to be on their side, but God's Word is the only fact. "He spake, and it was done; He commanded, and it stood fast." (Ps. xxxiii. 9.) So if every fact of your present experience is against the promise of God, still trust on, and you will soon find your experience confirm the Word of God if you hold on, *nothing wavering*.

"Thus saith the LORD; If My covenant be not with day and night, and if I have not appointed the ordinances of heaven and earth; Then will I cast away the seed of Jacob, and David My servant, so that I will not take any of his seed to be rulers over the seed of Abraham, Isaac, and Jacob: for I will cause their captivity to return, and have mercy on them."

Do you not think that I have proved my point that these three covenants are the backbone of the Old Testament; that every blessing, every future blessing and glory, rests upon these

THREE COVENANTS OF GRACE

with Noah, Abraham, and David?

With one more passage (Jer. xxxii. 38-44) we will close:

"And they shall be My people, and I will be

their God; and I will give them one heart, and one way, that they may fear Me for ever, for the good of them, and of their children after them: And I will make an everlasting covenant with them, that I will not turn away from them to do them good; but I will put My fear in their hearts, that they shall not depart from Me. Yea, I will rejoice over them to do them good, and I will plant them in this land assuredly with My whole heart, and with My whole soul. For thus saith the LORD; Like as I have brought all this great evil upon this people, so will I bring upon them all the good that I have promised them. And fields shall be bought in this land, whereof ye say, It is desolate without man or beast; it is given into the hands of the Chaldeans. Men shall buy fields for money, and subscribe evidences, and seal them, and take witnesses in the land of Benjamin, and in the places about Jerusalem, and in the cities of Judah, and in the cities of the mountains, and in the cities of the valley, and in the cities of the south: for I will cause their captivity to return, saith the LORD."

GLORY BE TO OUR FAITHFUL GOD!

II.

The Seed of the Woman.

And the LORD God said unto the serpent, ...
I will put enmity between thee and the woman, and between thy seed and her seed ; it shall bruise thy head, and thou shalt bruise his heel.

Genesis iii. 14, 15.

By Myself have I sworn, saith the LORD ; . . . .
in thy seed shall all the nations of the earth be blessed ;

Genesis xxii. 16, 18; xii. 3; xxvi. 4; xxviii. 14.

Now to Abraham and his seed were the promises made. He saith not And to seeds, as of many ; but as of one, And to thy seed, which is Christ.

Galatians iii. 16, 8.

The Seed of the Woman.

OUR foundation text (Gen. iii. 15) would read more literally thus:
"I will put enmity between thee and between the woman, and between thy seed and between her seed; He shall bruise thy head, and thou shalt bruise His heel."

This is God's first promise, and within that promise all the glory, all the grace, all the guidance, all the gifts that the world or the Church will ever get from God are enfolded; and they are unfolded as the ages roll on. Two sorts of seed are mentioned in these words; the seed of the serpent, which is very bad: and the seed of the woman, which is to be a man who in the end will destroy the serpent, for to bruise the head means to kill. "And thou shalt bruise his heel," that is, that the seed of the woman should undergo some suffering, some degradation, but would conquer in the end. And we see that the whole history of the world is made up of the enmity between the two seeds, the children of God and the children of the devil; and the reason that our world is in such a terrible state at present is that the children of the devil are free to have their own way, and the trail of the serpent seems to be over the politics, and the education, and all the social movements of the day. You cannot find a thing in this world which that trail has not defiled.

The next allusion to the seed of the woman which we will read is in Gen. iv. 25: Eve "bare a son, and called his name Seth: For God, said she, hath appointed me another seed instead of Abel, whom Cain slew." The following chapter gives us the genealogy of the family of Seth; then we come to the history of Noah and his three sons; and Gen. ix. 26, 27, tells us, " Blessed be the LORD God of Shem; and Canaan shall be his servant. God shall enlarge Japheth, and he shall dwell in the tents of Shem; and Canaan shall be his servant."

Here we get a narrowing down of the seed. We have had " the seed of the woman," then Seth, then Noah, and now God chooses Shem, as it is written: " Blessed of Jehovah, my God, be Shem," so that the seed of God through the woman is to be found in the line of Shem.

We pass on to Gen. xi., and find (verses 10 to 26) the generations of Shem, down to Terah. "And Terah lived seventy years, and begat Abram, Nahor, and Haran." And here again the election and sovereignty of God appear in choosing between these three brothers.

"Now Jehovah had said unto Abram, Get thee out of thy country, and from thy kindred, and from thy father's house, unto a land that I will show thee: And I will make of thee a great nation, and I will bless thee, and make thy name great; and thou shalt be a blessing. And I will bless them that bless thee, and curse him that curseth thee; and in thee shall all families of the earth be blessed." (Gen. xii. 1-3.)

These last words are quoted a great many times in the New Testament. In Acts iii. 25, that verse is called "the covenant." " Ye are the children of the prophets, and of the covenant which God made with our fathers, saying unto Abraham, And in thy seed shall all the kindreds of the earth be blessed." In Gal. iii. 8, it is called " the Gospel." " The Scripture, foreseeing that God would justify the heathen through faith, preached before the Gospel unto Abraham, saying, In thee shall all nations be blessed." And in verse 14, it is called "the blessing of Abraham," and in verse 17, "the promise," and in the 18th verse it is called "the inheritance;" so that this passage is one of the backbones of the Bible. Study it well if you want to deal with a Jew; study it on your knees with God, who calls it "the covenant," "the blessing of Abraham," "the promise," and "the inheritance."

Now we have come to Abraham and his seed; and we read how very impatient Abram was for God to fulfil to him His promise: and how, in his hurry he tried to force God to give him a son by Hagar; but God had told him that Sarah was to bear him a son, and after waiting twenty-five years, Isaac was born to him as by a miracle. The Jew, when talking of the miraculous birth of Christ, will say: 'I do not believe that a virgin had a son.' Our answer to that is, 'The whole Jewish nation is born of a miracle, Isaac was born by a miracle, the national life of Israel has been reared by miracles, the existence of the Jewish nation to-day is miraculous:' so it would be a strong argument against the Messiahship of Jesus if His birth were not miraculous, because God would then be acting contrary to all past precedent in the history of Israel.

In Gen. xxi. 1-6, and 12, we read: "The Lord visited Sarah as He had said, and the Lord did unto Sarah as He had spoken. For Sarah conceived, and bare Abraham a son in his old age, at the set time of which God had spoken to him. And Abraham called the name of his son that was born unto him, whom Sarah bare to him, Isaac," or "It is laughter." He was so filled with joy that he just laughed, for the fulfilment of God's promises to faith brings merriment and joy to the soul.

"And Abraham circumcised his son Isaac, being

eight days old, as God had commanded him. And Abraham was a hundred years old, when his son Isaac was born unto him. And Sarah said, God hath made me to laugh, so that all that hear will laugh with me."

"In Isaac shall thy seed be called."

Isaac had two sons; and of them we read (Gen. xxv. 27-34) that Esau despised his birthright: but Jacob, notwithstanding his natural meanness, set value upon the blessing; and by faith he reached out to the promise of the inheritance; and from among his twelve sons God chose that His purposes of grace should be manifested through the family of Judah.

"Judah, thou art he whom thy brethren shall praise; thy hand shall be in the neck of thine enemies; thy father's children shall bow down before thee. Judah is a lion's whelp; from the prey, my son, thou art gone up: he stooped down, he couched as a lion, and as an old lion; who shall rouse him up? The sceptre shall not depart from Judah, nor a lawgiver from between his feet, until Shiloh come; and unto Him shall the gathering of the people be:" or "unto Him shall the obedience of the people be." (Gen. xlix. 8-10.)

The word translated "sceptre" here is a word that throughout the Old Testament denotes "tribal staff," and the word translated "lawgiver" some authorities translate "prince," or "magistrate," and the meaning of the verse is this: That the tribal staff or tribal governor should not depart from Judah, nor the tribal ruler or magistrate from his posterity, until Shiloh come; or you may translate it "the man who is peace," and unto him shall the obedience of the people be. The tribe of Judah remained in its tribal condition until Jesus was born. The other tribes were lost, as it were, in Assyria, and no one knows exactly to this day where they are to be found; but

THE SEED OF THE WOMAN. 31

Judah retained its tribal condition and it gave laws to the children of Israel until Jesus came, until Shiloh came; and after they rejected Shiloh—the man who is peace—"the Prince of Peace," the tribe of Judah was scattered to the ends of the earth.

But Jesus shall come again, and unto Him shall the obedience of the people be. People may say, 'There are all these nations who do not obey Him; there are five hundred millions who have not heard of Him. There are only five hundred millions of baptised Christians who *nominally* bear His Name; so that even nominally the obedience of the people has not been unto Him.' But that verse shall have a literal fulfilment when great Shiloh comes back to bring peace to the earth: and because Jesus is away just now peace is away, and war is on the earth, and I think that before long we shall be deluged with war. You need no prophetic vision to see that there will be a terrible war before long; yea, there must be war upon the earth as long as our peace is in heaven.

Have you ever noticed how that is prophesied in the two anthems at the birth and the crucifixion of Jesus? (Luke ii. 14, xix. 38.) The anthem at His birth was this: "Glory to God in the highest, and on earth peace, good-will toward men." So peace came to earth in the person of Jesus; but just before Jesus left the earth His disciples began to praise Him on the Mount of Olives in these words: "Blessed be the King that cometh in the name of the Lord; peace in heaven, and glory in the highest." Peace was about to leave the earth and go back to heaven. The anthem of Christ's first advent told of peace coming down to the earth; but they rejected Him, and peace returned to heaven. But, praise God, peace is coming back again, and the time is near when the obedience of the nations shall belong to the Man of Peace at His second advent.

In tracing "the seed of the woman" in the family of Judah, we come down to the book of Ruth, chapter i.: "Now it came to pass, in the days when the judges ruled, that there was a famine in the land. And a certain man of Bethlehem-Judah went to sojourn in the country of Moab, he, and his wife, and his two sons."

Bethlehem-Judah! Here is the place where the promised seed was to be born. (Micah v. 2.)

"And Elimelech, Naomi's husband, died" there. You remember how afterwards Ruth clave to Naomi, and followed her back, and chose Jehovah as her God. And how Boaz noticed Ruth in his field, and exercised the right of the kinsman towards her, and bought Elimelech's portion, taking Ruth to be his wife; and how she bare a son, Obed, who was the father of Jesse, the father of David, the great king, through whom, by direct descent, the promised seed should come. (Ps. lxxxix. 4, 29, 36.)

Turning to another branch of this subject, let us look at Isa. vii. 14, and learn not only the *line* through which "the seed of the woman" must come, but the *nature* of that seed. "Behold, a virgin" (Hebrew, "the virgin") "shall conceive, and bear a son, and shall call His Name Immanuel," or "with us is God" —*i.e.*, the character of the Son to be born is this: He will be God manifest in the flesh, God with us.

If you want to learn something more about this wonderful child you will find it in Isaiah ix. 6: "For unto us"— that is, to the Jewish nation — "a child is born, unto us a Son is given." "God so loved the world, that He gave His only begotten Son, that whosoever believeth in Him should not perish, but have everlasting life." (John iii. 16.) The Son was given before He was born; He was given from eternity. Jesus is the true image of God. (Heb. i. 1-3.)

"And the government shall be upon His shoulder;" You know the fable of Atlas supporting the earth on his shoulders. Jesus is the true Atlas, and all the universe is upon His shoulders, and that is where His sheep also are carried. He took the lost sheep on His shoulders and carried it home. It is no more of a burden to Jesus to carry the universe than it is to carry a repentant child. The government of your life is upon His shoulder, though we are sorely tempted sometimes to take it away.

"And His Name"—that is, His character—"shall be called Wonderful." You do not understand Christ unless He does something wonderful for you. His character is not changed. His Name still is Wonderful, always Wonderful, and if your faith reaches out to Him, He will do wonderful things for you.

He is also called "Counsellor," and if ever there were days in which we needed counsel it is in these last days of the nineteenth century. So take counsel from God in every little thing, because great results may depend upon little things. Great men may come to you, as the Gibeonites came to Joshua, pretending to be what they are not. They may come with garments that are old, and bread that is rotten in their hands, and they say they come from a far country, and they look very respectable and real, but when you take counsel of God you will see through them, and God will show you the right thing to do.

And also this child is to be "the mighty God, the everlasting Father," or "the Father of the Ages," for God has constructed the ages in reference to Jesus His Son, and so He is "the Father of Eternity." All eternity, as manifested to man, has reference to Jesus, whether past or future. And He is "the Prince of Peace. Of the increase of His government and peace there shall be no end, upon the throne of David, and upon His kingdom, to order it, and to establish it with judgment and with justice from henceforth even for ever." Well might we sink down under such a prospect and weight of glory: but these words are given to encourage us: " The zeal of the LORD of hosts will perform this." (Comp. 2 Kings xix. 31; Isa. xxxvii. 32.)

Turn now to Isa. xi. for a description of this Son of David: "And there shall come forth a rod out of the stem of Jesse, and a Branch shall grow out of His roots; and the Spirit of the Lord shall rest upon Him, the spirit of wisdom and understanding, the spirit of counsel and might, the spirit of knowledge and of the fear of the Lord; and shall make Him of quick understanding in the fear of the Lord;" (Hebrew, "quick scent in the fear of Jehovah") Yes, Jesus is quick to detect the very smallest dereliction or straying from the path of God's will. He recognises sin at once. " I know thy works." " I am He which searcheth the reins and hearts ; and I will give unto every one of you according to your works." " Thou hast left thy first love." (Rev. ii. 4, 19, 23.) He is quick of scent in the sight of Jehovah; and let us remember that we have to do with the Lord Jesus Christ, Who means us to be sensitive too.

"And He shall not judge after the sight of His eyes," that is, according to outward appearance. Samuel judged by outward appearance when he saw the sons of Jesse. (1 Sam. xvi.) When Eliab was brought before him he thought he looked well as regards his countenance and height, and Samuel said, " Surely the Lord's anointed is before Him." ' No,' said the Lord, ' he is not My anointed,' "for the LORD seeth not as man seeth; for man looketh on the outward appearance, but the LORD looketh on the heart." So Samuel had to pass by Eliab and the other brothers until he came to David, who was a keeper of sheep, and whose heart was busy with God in the desert. He was, in God's energy, defending the sheep against lions and bears. Such a person God chose. So neither God the Father nor God the Son ever judged by outward appearance.

"Neither reprove after the hearing of His ears." That is, if one of us tells a story against another, and Jesus hears it—and He *does* hear it—Jesus will not reprove you or me for the sin with which we are charged: "But with righteousness shall He judge the poor, and reprove with equity for the meek of the earth: and He shall smite the earth with the rod of His mouth, and with the breath of His lips shall He slay the wicked." There is an exact quotation of that verse in 2 Thess. ii. 8: "And then shall that wicked be revealed, whom the Lord shall consume with the spirit of His mouth, and shall destroy with the brightness of His coming." It is the same word that is used for breath and spirit in Hebrew with which He will destroy the wicked one. It is singular there, not plural, so that chapter looks on to the destruction of the deceiver, Anti-Christ, by the manifestation of Jesus from heaven, when He appears in His glory to reign.

"And righteousness shall be the girdle of His loins, and faithfulness the girdle of His reins."

Now peace is once more come to the earth, therefore "The wolf also shall dwell with the lamb, and the leopard shall lie down with the kid; and the calf, and the young lion, and the fatling together; and a little child shall lead them. And the cow and the bear shall feed; their young ones shall lie down together: and the lion shall eat straw like the ox." That is, all the natural fierce propensities of the wild animals shall cease during the millennial reign of Christ. We shall not then be afraid to go into a dark forest, for should we see a lion there we can go and pat him, and the same with a tiger ; and if we feel tired we can go and rest our head upon him.

"And the sucking child shall play on the hole of the asp, and the weaned child shall put his hand on the cockatrice' den." The serpent will not be allowed to bite them. "They shall not hurt nor destroy in all My holy mountain : for the earth shall be full of the knowledge of the Lord, as the waters cover the sea." What a grand time is coming ! Oh, how we ought to pray, "Thy kingdom come, Thy will be done in earth as it is in heaven." The Lord's Prayer is far from being fully answered yet, but it must be fulfilled. (Matt. vi. 10.)

"And in that day there shall be a root of Jesse," He is not only a rod or Branch springing from David as the son of David, but He is the very root out of which David himself sprang. David himself would never have had existence but that Jesus had existence. And this root of Jesse " shall stand for an ensign of the people ; to it shall the Gentiles seek ; and His rest shall be glorious." Or, more literally, "glory." When Jesus rests and is satisfied, glory shall cover the earth.

He "shall stand for an ensign of the people ;" that is, be lifted up, as you lift up things upon a staff to show them clearly. Moses made a serpent of brass and lifted it up as an ensign for the people to see. So Jesus has been lifted up for the whole world to see, and "to Him shall the Gentiles seek, and His rest shall be glory." (See John iii. 14-18: xii. 32, 33.)

"And it shall come to pass in that day, that the Lord shall set His hand again the second time to recover the remnant of His people, which shall be left, from Assyria, and from Egypt, and from Pathros, and from Cush, (that is, Ethiopia) and from Elam,

(Persia) and from Shinar, and from Hamath, and from the islands of the sea. And He shall set up an ensign for the nations, and shall assemble the outcasts of Israel, and gather together the dispersed of Judah from the four corners of the earth. The envy also of Ephraim shall depart, and the adversaries of Judah shall be cut off; Ephraim shall not envy Judah, and Judah shall not vex Ephraim. And there shall be an highway for the remnant of His people, which shall be left, from Assyria; like as it was to Israel in the day that he came up out of the land of Egypt."

This shows us that there will be great wonders and signs done again in this dispensation; for the return of Israel to Palestine is to be *like as it was* when they came out of Egypt, when God multiplied His signs and wonders, and brought them forth with a strong hand and with a stretched-out arm. (See Ex. iii. 20; vi. 6; vii. 3; xi. 9.)

See further in Isa. xlii. 1-7: "Behold, My servant, whom I uphold, Mine Elect, in whom My soul delighteth: I have put My Spirit upon Him; He shall bring forth judgment to the Gentiles," or, "to the nations." Judgment constantly means justice.

"He shall not cry, nor lift up, nor cause His voice to be heard in the street."

That is, He will not act in a violent way; He will not assert Himself; for there will be such power that He will act quietly. Real power always acts quietly. If I asked a little child to lift up that chair he would pull and tug at it, and get it up a few inches; but if I ask that muscular young man to lift it he would do it easily. Real power does not exert itself. Jesus is the power of God, and He will soon appear in the world, and wrongs will be put right before we know where we are. He will speak for the Spirit of the Lord is upon Him.

But although He is so powerful, He is mightily gentle. "A bruised reed shall He not break, and the smoking flax shall He not quench." If you ever smelt smoking flax you know how unpleasant it is: yet He will not put out smoking flax.

"He shall bring forth judgment unto truth. He shall not fail nor be discouraged, till He have set judgment in the earth: and the isles shall wait for His law. Thus saith God Jehovah, He that created the heavens, and stretched them out; He that spread forth the earth, and that which cometh out of it; He that giveth breath unto the people upon it, and spirit to them that walk therein; I Jehovah have called Thee in righteousness, and will hold Thine hand, and will keep Thee, and give Thee for a covenant of the people, for a light of the Gentiles."

The three covenants mentioned in our last Reading are fulfilled in Christ, therefore Christ Himself is here called Covenant. "The people" is singular, and refers to the Jews. He is a covenant to Israel, but He never made a covenant with the nations. Any blessing we have we get through the Jews; so let us not become wise in our own conceits. "For if thou wert cut out of the olive tree, which is wild by nature, and wert graffed contrary to nature into a good olive tree, how much more shall these, which be the natural branches, be graffed into their own olive tree? For I would not, brethren, that ye should be ignorant of this mystery, lest ye should be wise in your own conceits; that blindness in part is happened to Israel, until the fulness of the Gentiles be come in." (Rom. xi. 24, 25.) So the nations in their own conceits are despising the Jews, and the poor Jews are outcasts; but God is going to teach the nations not to despise the Jews. "And in that day will I make Jerusalem a burdensome stone for all people: all that burden themselves with it shall be cut in pieces, though all the people of the earth be gathered together against it." (Zech. xii. 3.) Jerusalem will become a burdensome stone to the politicians of Europe, and they will not know what to do with Palestine.

Let us, before closing this subject, look at that wonderful description of Jehovah's servant in Isa. lii. and liii : " Behold, My servant shall deal prudently," or, " prosper," as in Josh. i. 8 and in Ps. i. 3. " He shall be exalted and extolled, and be very high. As many were astonished at Thee ; His visage was so marred more than any man, and His form more than the sons of men ; " That is, He seemed perhaps so downcast, and humble, and meek, and to make no pretension that they were astonished at Him.

"So shall He sprinkle many nations ;" The word translated "sprinkle" there may also be translated "astonish." Then it reads: "As many were astonished at Thee ; . . . . so shall He cause many nations to be astonished."

"The kings shall shut their mouths at Him : for that which had not been told them shall they see, and that which they had not heard shall they consider. Who hath believed our report? and to whom is the arm of the LORD revealed? For He shall grow up before Him as a tender plant, and as a root out of a dry ground: He hath no form nor comeliness; and when we (that is, Israel) shall see Him, there is no beauty that we should desire Him."

There is no manifestation of outward glory in Him, so that worldly people should desire Him.

" He is despised and rejected of men ;"—that is true of Jesus of Nazareth—"a man of sorrows, and acquainted with grief: and we hid as it were our faces from Him ; He was despised, and we esteemed Him not. Surely He hath borne our griefs, and carried our sorrows : yet we did esteem Him stricken.

smitten of God, and afflicted." That is, we thought He died such a miserable death that He could not be a Servant of God at all, but was smitten by God in judgment.

"But He was wounded for our transgressions, He was bruised for our iniquities: the chastisement of our peace was upon Him;" or, "the chastisements which procured our peace were upon Him;" "and with His stripes we are healed. All we like sheep have gone astray; we have turned every one to his own way; and Jehovah caused to meet on Him the iniquity of us all."

That verse begins and ends with the same word in the original. It is wonderful the pathos and sorrow that breathe through it in Hebrew. "And the Lord laid on Him the iniquity of *all we*."

"He was oppressed," or, more literally, "It was exacted," that the law should be magnified. The last claim of God's law upon a sinner was exacted from the Messiah, because He took our place, and "He becometh answerable." "And He was afflicted, yet He opened not His mouth:" He did not accuse His father of injustice; He accepted, for us, the curse to the full.

"He is brought as a lamb to the slaughter, and as a sheep before her shearers is dumb, so He openeth not His mouth. He was taken from prison and from judgment." Justice was not allowed Him by His enemies; He was condemned unjustly.

"And who shall declare His generation?" That is a very difficult sentence; it may mean, "Who shall declare the mystery of His eternal generation?" or, "Who can describe the character of that evil generation that rejected Him, the generation that robbed Him of all justice, and spat upon Him, and crucified the Son of God; who shall declare that generation?"

"For He was cut off out of the land of the living: for the transgression of My people was He stricken. And He made His grave with the lawless ones, and with the rich man in His deaths;" It is wonderful that the word "death" is in the plural here. The only explanation is that all deaths are included in His. "And He made His deaths with the rich man, because He had done no violence, neither was any deceit in His mouth. Yet it pleased the LORD to bruise Him;" That is, to put Him to death, as we saw He would do to the serpent: "He will bruise the serpent's head." "He hath put Him to grief: When Thou shalt make His soul a trespass offering for sin." In Lev. xvii. 11 we read, "It is the blood that maketh an atonement for the soul." The Hebrew is, "It is the blood that maketh an atonement through the life, for the life is in the blood."

"He shall see His seed, He shall prolong His days, and the pleasure of the LORD shall prosper in His hand. He shall see of the travail of His soul, and shall be satisfied:"

It will take a great deal to satisfy the soul of Jesus after all His sufferings; but they have proved to be the birth-pangs of the Church of the living God. As each soul is born into eternal life through the Spirit and the Word, the heart of Jesus rejoices: and in the salvation of His people Israel, and of us "sinners of the Gentiles," He will be supremely satisfied.

"By His knowledge shall My righteous Servant justify many; for He shall bear their iniquities. Therefore will I divide Him a portion with the great, and He shall divide the spoil with the strong; because He hath poured out his life unto death: and He was numbered with the transgressors, and He bare the sin of many, and continueth to make intercession for the transgressors." (Hebrews vii. 25.) "Wherefore He is able also to save them to the uttermost that come unto God by Him, seeing He ever liveth to make intercession for them."

III.

A Prophet like unto Moses.

The LORD thy God will raise up unto thee a Prophet from the midst of thee, of thy brethren, like unto me ; unto him ye shall hearken ;

. . . .

I will raise them up a Prophet from among their brethren, like unto thee, and will put My words in his mouth ; and he shall speak unto them all that I command him.

And it shall come to pass that whosoever will not hearken unto My words which he shall speak in My name, I will require it of him.

Deuteronomy xviii. 15, 18, 19.

.

I have given unto them the words which Thou gavest Me ; and they have received them, and have known surely that I came out from Thee, and they have believed that Thou didst send Me.

The words of Jesus in John xvii. 8.

A Prophet like unto Moses.

THE reason I believe in the New Testament is that it is a continuation of the Old Testament. That is what the Chinaman thought when he received a New Testament from a missionary. He brought it back and said, 'Please, sir, this seems to be the continuation of another book; where is the first volume?' 'Yes,' said the missionary, 'there is another volume, and I can give it you: there is the Old Testament in Chinese for you.' Oh! yes, thank God, there is another volume, and there are many things that I could not understand but for that volume. The Lord Jesus said Moses "wrote of Me, but if ye believe not his writings, how shall ye believe My words?" (John v. 46, 47.) That is the reason why faith in Christ is declining amongst many learned people to-day—because they are ceasing to believe in the writings of Moses. And when you cease to believe in the five Books of Moses you lose your faith in Christ. So I want to compare these Old Testament sayings with what is said of Jesus Christ in the New Testament, and to commend them to every man's conscience. God has given you a conscience to discern the truth, like a peal of bells. Do you know how a tuner finds out a note on a deep peal of bells? He sounds a note on a higher octave, and when he comes to the corresponding note the bell answers to it. So your conscience has music in it, and it responds to truth, and when the truth of God is sounded, your conscience will re-echo to it; there will be a response in your heart saying, 'What that man says is true.' So it will be with what Jesus says. You must have a sound heart in order to hear His truth.

There are a great many people who come to our churches whose hearts are like cracked bells. They may listen to the Gospel until doomsday without its doing them any good; and it does not do you any good until you want to know about your sins and your need of a Saviour, for it is then you begin to be true, and you say, 'That is the very thing for me; it suits me exactly.'

Let us take as a foundation text for our subject to-night Deut. xviii. 18, 19:

"I will raise them up a Prophet from among their brethren, like unto thee, and will put My words in his mouth; and he shall speak unto them all that I shall command him. And it shall come to pass that whosoever will not hearken unto My words, which he shall speak in My name, I will require it of him."

Now, a prophet is a person who tells forth the will of God and the truth of God to the people. Prediction of coming events is no necessary element in the conception of a prophet. The word simply means "to tell forth," and as what God says has constantly a reference to the future, the word has acquired the meaning of the prediction of coming events. So now we want you to consider Moses as the greatest prophet, and then to see how like he was to Jesus, and that Jesus of Nazareth is the only person who answers to the description of Moses. "I will raise up a Prophet from among their brethren like unto thee."

Moses was the greatest of the prophets. We

read in Deut. xxxiv. 10, "And there arose not a prophet since in Israel like unto Moses, whom the Lord knew face to face." Now, those words were written, as the Jews themselves say, by Ezra: he added that note to Deut. xxxiv., therefore that clears my way considerably, for there is the testimony of a Jewish scribe—an inspired man—that up to 455 B.C. no prophet had risen "like unto Moses." Therefore it is in vain to search the Old Testament for a prophet like unto Moses: and no one will claim that such a prophet arose between the time of Ezra and the advent of Jesus Christ, for prophecy ceased with Malachi; and my work to-night is to show that the Lord Jesus Christ, and the Lord Jesus Christ *only*, answers to those words of Moses.

Now, I want to give good reasons for that statement.

One thing I note about Moses is this: That God appointed him to be the Redeemer of His people Israel from Egypt.

For fully two hundred and fifteen years the people had been in Egypt, and the taskmaster's whip had been descending on their shoulders, and their cry rose up to God because of their cruel bondage, and God said, 'I do remember My covenant with Abraham, and Isaac, and Jacob, and I have come down to deliver My people Israel from the hands of the Egyptians, and to bring them up out of that land unto a good land and a large, unto a land flowing with milk and honey. Now, Moses, come, and I will send thee unto Pharaoh, that thou mayest bring forth My people, the children of Israel, out of Egypt.' (See Ex ii. iii. and vi.) So God chose Moses to be the redeemer of Israel, and through what Moses did and said, in the power and under the guidance of God, that nation was born in a day; that nation of slaves on Passover night became a nation of free people; Israel's free life began on that Passover night, and Moses was used of God for their redemption.

No prophet has risen since to answer to that characteristic but Jesus Christ; He is the only one who lays claim to redeem people; the only one mighty in word and mighty in deed; the Lord Jesus Christ is able to deliver people from all bondage. I would not stand upon this platform to-night unless I knew that twenty-one years ago He brought me out from under the bondage of sin, and He spoke peace to my soul, and His joy and peace have been there ever since. So we desire to speak that we do know, and testify that we have seen, and heard, and felt concerning the Word of Life, that the Lord Jesus is indeed a great Redeemer and Saviour. Oh! it is a glad thing to be able to say, 'The Lord has redeemed me from slavery; He has put His liberty in my soul; I am one of God's people; the very nature of God is within me; I have become a partaker of the Divine nature.' (See Tit. ii. 14; 2 Pet. i. 4; Rev. v. 9.) And as Moses was the redeemer of Israel from bondage, so Jesus is the Redeemer of His people from sin. As was said by the angel Gabriel, "Thou shalt call His name JESUS: for He shall save His people from their sins." (Matt. i. 21.) Have you been saved from your sins? Is there one here to-night who does not know what it is to be saved from sin?

> Full salvation! full salvation!
> From the guilt and power of sin!

Secondly, Moses was a Mediator between God and man. It says so in our chapter, verse 16:

"According to all that thou desiredst of the LORD

thy God in Horeb in the day of the assembly, saying, Let me not hear again the voice of the LORD my God, neither let me see this great fire any more, that I die not. And the LORD said unto me, They have well spoken that which they have spoken. I will raise them up a Prophet from among their brethren, like unto thee, and will put My words in His mouth, and He shall speak unto them all that I shall command Him."

When the people came to Mount Sinai the mountain was burning with fire, and the smoke ascended as the smoke of a furnace, and the lightnings flashed, and the thunders were rolling over the plain, and the people trembled; and above all that rose the voice of God, like a trumpet, and it waxed louder and louder, and even Moses said, "I exceedingly fear and quake." (Heb. xii. 21.) The people then said unto Moses, "Go thou up unto God; speak thou with us, and we will hear; but let not God speak with us, lest we die." (See Ex. xx. 19; Deut. v. 27.) Then God commanded Moses to come up to Him, and Moses went up, and for forty days he was surrounded by the glory of God, and the living God spoke to him, and his soul was filled with glory, and his face was radiant with peace, and his heart filled with the love of God. Then he came down and gave the law of God—the perfect law —to the people. Moses was therefore a mediator between God and the people of Israel. Moses told the people God's words. He received them from God and told them to the people.

Now, that is just what Jesus does. If our sense of sin is keen, we feel uncomfortable about prayer. You ask a man to pray when he is conscious of having done wrong, conscious of sin, and he can't. He says, 'I cannot pray. How do I know God will hear my prayer?' And when we feel in that way we at once say, 'Oh! that I had someone to come between God and me; someone to present my case to God! Oh! that I had someone to intercede for me!' So the great and awful God has veiled Himself in human flesh, and He has appointed the Lord Jesus Christ, His only Son, to act for us, and now he that has seen Jesus has seen the Eternal Father. If you want to know what God the Father is, study the four Gospels, for whatever Jesus is, that is what the Eternal God is this moment. Oh! study the heart of Jesus! "There is one God, and one Mediator between God and men, the man Christ Jesus." (1 Tim. ii. 5.) He, having the Divine nature, can lay His hand upon God, and say, "Father, I represent Thee"; and having human nature, He can lay His hand upon us, and say, "Father, I represent that man; let Thy words pass to him through Me."

Have you a Mediator? "I am the Way, and the Truth, and the Life; no man cometh unto the Father but by Me." (John xiv. 6.) So whenever the people of Israel wanted anything, they referred it to Moses, and Moses told God, and God gave the answer to Moses, who delivered it to the people. The Lord spoke to other prophets in dreams and visions, but it was not so with His servant Moses. "The Lord spake unto Moses face to face, as a man speaketh unto his friend." (Ex. xxxiii. 11.) So with the Lord Jesus; God speaks to Him face to face. Oh! it is a glorious thought, that *now*, while I am speaking here, my Blessed Saviour is face to face with God, and is aware of what is going on at Paddington Baths. This meeting is interesting to Him because He is interested in the salvation of His brethren.

Thirdly, Moses was the Law-giver. He gave the people laws and statutes. He gave them in God's name It was the same as if God had spoken to them. "He shall speak words in My name." Now, the Lord Jesus lays claim to this: that every word He spoke was His Father's word. Listen to this: "The word which ye hear is not Mine, but the Father's which sent Me." (John xiv. 24). "I have given unto them the words which Thou gavest me; and they have received them." (xvii. 8). "As My Father hath taught Me, I speak these things." (viii. 28). "For I have not spoken of Myself; but the Father which sent Me, He gave Me a commandment, what I should say, and what I should speak. . . . Whatsoever I speak therefore, even as the Father said unto Me, so I speak." (xii. 49, 50). Here Jesus says that every word that He uttered the Eternal Father spoke it in Him and through Him. Now, that is an awful claim to make. Any man that would make such a claim as that *falsely* would deserve to have his name branded with eternal infamy. "Whatsoever I say unto you"—I, Jesus of Nazareth, I who have worked as a carpenter for thirty years—"Whatsoever I say, God the Father saith it. He doeth My works. I and My Father are one." No wonder the Jews took up stones to stone Him. "Why do ye stone Me?" He asked. They answered, "For a good work we stone Thee not; but for blasphemy; and because that Thou, being a man, makest Thyself God." (x. 33.) They saw the point at once. All His works were the Father's works; He spoke no words but the Father's words; He had no thoughts but the Father's thoughts; there was no distinction between Him and the Eternal God. They saw at once that He claimed Divinity. So Jesus has given us the words of the eternal and living God, and this (holding up the Bible) is indeed the Word of God.

Do you believe that every word in that Book is the word of God to your soul? Oh! what consolation it is when you can take this Book from Genesis to Revelation and know it is the Word of God to your heart, not a mixture of truth and error, but truth, undiluted truth, and truth purified seven times in the fire. And so, as God spoke, Moses spoke; as God speaks, so Jesus speaks. He speaks the very words of God. For example, in the Sermon on the Mount notice how the Lord speaks of the fulfilment of the law. "Think not that I am come to destroy the law. . . . I am not come to destroy, but to fulfil. For verily I say unto you, Till heaven and earth pass, one jot or one tittle shall in no wise pass from the law, till all be fulfilled." (Matt. v. 17, 18.) And then the Lord Jesus goes on to show us how the law of Moses was perfectly fulfilled in His teaching; how it cannot be fulfilled unless it is fulfilled in spirit as well as in outward act. God requires it to be fulfilled within you. Your inner being must be in harmony with the law before you can fulfil it.

Now, notice how the Lord Jesus teaches the fulfilment of the law. "Ye have heard that it was said by them of old time, Thou shalt not kill; and whosoever shall kill shall be in danger of the judgment. But I say unto you, That whosoever is angry with his brother without a cause shall be in danger of the judgment;" for in spirit he may then be guilty of murder. I must beware not only of murder, but of the smallest angry feeling in my soul, lest I become a murderer. The Lord Jesus saves from that. He is such a wonderful Saviour that He can deliver me from feeling angry, and from the least internal irritation. You will be tempted to irritation, of course, but He can say, 'Thus far shall it go, and no further.' Any man who is angry with his brother without a cause is a murderer, and "no murderer hath eternal life abiding in him." Then there is the *law of purity*. If you allow a lustful thought in your soul you have committed adultery already. Then He gives commands about divorce, making the law of divorce more stringent than the law of Moses. Moses, because of the hardness of their hearts, had allowed them to write a bill of divorcement. "But I say unto you, That whosoever shall put away his wife, saving for the cause of fornication, causeth her to commit adultery; and whosoever shall marry her that is divorced committeth adultery. Again, ye have heard that it hath been said by them of old time, Thou shalt not forswear thyself, but shalt perform unto the Lord thine oaths. But I say unto you, Swear not at all; neither by heaven, for it is God's throne; nor by the earth, for it is His footstool; neither by Jerusalem, for it is the city of the great King; neither shalt thou swear by thy head, because thou canst not make one hair white or black. But let your communication be Yea, yea; Nay, nay. For whatsoever is more than these, cometh of evil."

Oh! may God give us grace to say "Yes" when we mean yes, and "No" when we mean no.

Then, "Ye have heard that it hath been said, An eye for an eye and a tooth for a tooth. But I say unto you, That ye resist not evil; but whosoever shall smite thee on thy right cheek, turn to him the other also. And if any man will sue thee at the law, and take away thy coat, let him have thy cloak also. And whosoever shall compel thee to go a mile, go with him twain. Give to him that asketh thee, and from him that would borrow of thee turn not thou away."

But, you say, 'I would have nothing left!' Just ask God how to put those things in practice, and He will tell you.

"Ye have heard that it hath been said, Thou

shalt love thy neighbour and hate thine enemy. But I say unto you, Love your enemies, bless them that curse you, do good to them that hate you, and pray for them which despitefully use you and persecute you, that ye may be the children of your Father which is in heaven; for He maketh His sun to rise on the evil and on the good, and sendeth rain on the just and on the unjust. For if ye love them which love you, what reward have ye? Do not even the publicans the same? And if ye salute your brethren only, what do ye more than others? Do not even the publicans so? Be ye therefore perfect, even as your Father which is in heaven is perfect."

Thus the Lord Jesus Christ is our Law-giver. He says on His own authority, "Such and such was said of old time, but now I, the fulness of the law, have come into the world, the darkness is passing away, the True Light now shineth, *I say unto thee.*" The Lord is our Law-giver, the Lord is our Judge. May God teach us the spiritual meaning of Christ's law, and teach us to fulfil it in the power of the Holy Ghost.

In Deut. xxxiii. 5. Moses is called a King. We read: "Moses commanded us a law, even the inheritance of the congregation of Jacob. And he was king in Jeshurun" (Jeshurun is a poetical expression for Israel) "when the heads of the people and the tribes of Israel were gathered together." And no one, certainly, will answer to that description but the Lord Jesus Christ. He is the only one who has claimed to be King of the Jews, as well as Prophet and Priest. Jesus is King, and the time will quickly come when the Lord will set His King upon His holy hill of Zion. (Ps. ii. 6.)

Another point. Moses was at first rejected by Israel—by Israel whom he came to save. He saw two men of the Hebrews fighting, and he asked the one who did the wrong, "Wherefore smitest thou thy fellow?" And the man who did his neighbour wrong turned round and said, "Who made thee a prince and a judge over us?" (Ex. ii. 13, 14.) They rejected Moses. He thought they would understand, but they did not. It is like Israel now. Jesus came and offered Himself to Israel, but they rejected Him. "He was despised and rejected of men; a man of sorrows and acquainted with grief; and we (Israel) hid as it were our faces from Him. He was despised, and we esteemed Him not. . . . We (Israel) did esteem Him stricken, smitten of God, and afflicted. But He was wounded for our transgressions." (Is. liii. 3-5.) The time is quickly coming (and because it is quickly coming we hold these meetings) when the Lord Jesus, the King of Israel, will appear, and when the whole nation of Israel will be "born in a day," and they shall look upon Him "whom they have pierced, and they shall mourn for Him as one mourneth for his only son, and shall be in bitterness for Him, as one that is in bitterness for his first-born." (Zech. xii. 10.) The rejected One will come again, and will be crowned with glory and honour, and He must reign until all enemies are put under His feet.

Another mark about Moses. He gave up his princely position—yea, gave up all that he had, in order to save his people Israel. He had been adopted into Pharaoh's house; he had the treasures of Egypt at his feet; he was mighty in word and deed; he was one of the first warriors of the day; but when he came to years of discretion he said, 'The promise of God to my father Abraham is more to me than all the glory and treasures in Egypt.' "He had respect unto the recompense of the reward." He chose "rather to suffer affliction with the people of God than to enjoy the pleasures of sin for a season; esteeming the reproach of Christ greater riches than the treasures in Egypt; for he had respect unto the recompense of the reward." (Heb. xi. 25.) What faith! And we need the same now. Some would in those days come up to him and say, 'Moses, why do you act like this? You are going to give up your chance of the throne; you are going to give up the glory of Egypt; you are going to give up a position in which your word is law in the whole of Egypt; you are going to give up all for the sake of some obscure promise that your tribal God made to a nation of slaves. Your God cannot even bring His people out of slavery. Why, they have almost forgotten His name. Our gods are much better. Look at the magnificent temple of Isis; look at the temples of Thebes; look at the colossal statues. Your God is never seen. What a fool you are, Moses!' Of course people spoke in that way; but he esteemed the reproach for the hope of the Messiah greater riches than the treasures in Egypt.

And that is how they speak to-day. If you go out of this hall to-night with your souls on fire and your hearts blazing and determined to go through thick and thin for God in your offices, your places of business, and everywhere else, I can tell you you will come in for reproach too. They will say, 'What nonsense to go on like this. It is utter fanaticism.' But you know in your soul the Lord Jesus is more valuable to you than ever before. His peace is flowing through your heart.

So Moses gave up all. He suffered the loss of all things for his people Israel. And what did our Lord Jesus Christ give up? He was at the right hand of the Father. It was the word of Jesus that made the world, and yet He said, 'Father, I lay down My life at Thy feet, that I may take it again. Father, let Me go down to that world; let Me be born of that pure Jewish Virgin; let Me be clothed in a garment of flesh, that I may save My people Israel and a lost world.' And the Father said, 'Go.' And so, when the fulness of time came, Jesus was born of a woman. He was born under the law, that He might "redeem them that were under the law, that we might receive the adoption of sons." (Gal. iv. 4, 5.) So the Lord Jesus, my Saviour, gave up all for us men, and for our salvation. "He emptied Himself, and took upon Him the form of a servant, and was made in the likeness of men; and being found in fashion as a man, He humbled Himself, and became obedient unto death, even the death of the Cross. Wherefore God also hath highly exalted Him, and given Him a name which is above every name." (Phil. ii. 7, 8, 9.)

What have you ever lost for the sake of Jesus? Have you ever suffered in reputation, in your pocket, in your health for the sake of Jesus Christ? Have you ever lost anything for His sake? Paul could say, "I have suffered the loss of all things for the excellency of the knowledge of Christ Jesus my Lord." And Paul says, "Be ye followers of me, even as I also am of Christ." (See Phil. iii. 7, 8; 1 Cor. xi. 1.)

And I may add another point. Have you ever thought of the death of Moses? Where did Moses die? It is very remarkable what the Scripture says about that. The Scripture says that God buried Moses over against Beth-peor. Now, Beth-peor was the scene of Israel's most shameful sin, the scene of Israel's deepest degradation, when the wrath of God went forth and slew twenty-four thousand by the plague in one day, because of their whoredom and idolatry with the people of Moab. (See Num. xxv.; Josh. xxii. 17; Ps. cvi. 28; Hosh. ix. 10.) And over against the scene of Israel's sin Moses was buried by God. Some ancient Jewish Rabbis said that God buried Moses over against Beth-peor in order to atone for Israel's sin? They did not see the force of their remark. Our Lord Jesus Christ died, not on Nebo or Pisgah, but on Calvary, over against Jerusalem, where Israel had just rejected Him as their Messiah and King, and His body was buried, after making true atonement for the sins of the whole world.

God watched over the body of Moses. We read that Satan contended for the body of Moses, probably to turn it to corruption: but God kept it, that it might appear in glory with Elijah on the Mount of Transfiguration. (See Jude 9; and Matt. xvii. 3.) In like manner the body of Jesus was kept from corruption. "Thou wilt not suffer Thine Holy One to see corruption." (Ps. xvi. 10.) So on the third day after His crucifixion the body of Jesus was raised beyond the power of weakness and death, and in "the power of an endless life." (See Acts ii. 22-36; Heb. vii. 16.)

There is one more solemn point, with which I close. What did our text say?

"And it shall come to pass, that whosoever will not hearken unto My words, which He shall speak in My name, I will require it of him."

Now, the man who disregarded "Moses' law died without mercy, under two or three witnesses. Of how much sorer punishment, suppose ye, shall he be thought worthy who hath trodden under foot the Son of God, and hath counted the blood of the covenant, wherewith he was sanctified, an unholy thing, and hath done despite unto the Spirit of

Grace?" (Heb. x. 28, 29.) It was an awful thing to reject the words of Moses. How much more awful, says the Apostle, will it be to reject the words of Jesus! The rejection of Moses will bring upon you the first death; the rejection of the word of Jesus will bring upon you "the second death," when soul and body will be destroyed. "Whosoever believeth in Him shall not perish, but have everlasting life." "He that believeth on Him (Jesus) is not condemned, but he that believeth not is condemned already, because he hath not believed in the name of the only begotten Son of God." "He that believeth on the Son hath everlasting life, and he that believeth not the Son shall not see life, but the wrath of God abideth on him." (John iii. 16, 18, 36.) And those who reject the Lord Jesus to the bitter, bitter end, when He comes again in His glory, and His holy angels with Him, shall receive punishment, even eternal destruction, from the presence of the Lord. Oh! how earnestly we should plead with those who are rejecting the words of the "greater than Moses." If a man hears the words of this Prophet and rejects them, God will require it of him. What were some of the last words of Jesus to the Jews? Listen.

"If any man hear My words, and believe not, I judge him not:"—that is, I judge him not now—"for I came not to judge the world, but to save the world. He that rejecteth Me, and receiveth not My words, hath One that judgeth him: the word that I have spoken, the same shall judge him in the last day. For I have not spoken of Myself, but the Father which sent Me, He gave Me a commandment what I should say and what I should speak. And I know that His commandment is life everlasting: whatsoever I speak, therefore, even as the

Father said unto Me, so I speak." (John xii. 47-50.)

I will now sum up the points.

First of all, Christ is like Moses because Christ is the Redeemer of His people.

Christ is like Moses because Christ is the Mediator of His people.

Christ is like Moses because He is the Lawgiver of His people.

Christ is like Moses because Christ is King. He reigns over and rules His people.

Christ is like Moses because Moses was first of all rejected by Israel, and Christ is now rejected by His own flesh and blood.

Moses gave up all he had for his people, and Christ gave up all He had with the Father before the foundation of the world in order to save us from sin and its consequences.

The body of Jesus was kept from corruption, and He was raised from the dead on the third day.

Moses also appeared in glory with Elijah, and, praise be to God, the Lord Jesus will soon appear in glory again. He is coming to give a reward to those who are faithful to Him. God grant that each one here may surrender spirit, soul, and body to the One greater than Moses, and may all that you have be His from this night, and for evermore. Amen.

IV.

An Eternal Priest.

And Melchizedek, King of Salem, brought forth bread and wine : and he was the priest of the Most High God.

Genesis xiv. 18.

The LORD hath sworn, and will not repent, Thou art a priest for ever after the order of Melchizedek.

Psalm cx. 4.

... After the similitude of Melchizedek there ariseth another priest,

Who is made, not after the law of a carnal commandment, but after the power of an endless life. For He testifieth, Thou art a priest for ever after the order of Melchizedek.

Hebrews vii. 15, 16, 17.

An Eternal Priest.

THE LORD "will not repent," *i.e.*, will not change His purpose.

Let us read Gen. xiv. 17-24:

"And the king of Sodom went out to meet him (Abram) after his return from the slaughter of Chedorlaomer, and of the kings that were with him, at the valley of Shaveh, which is the king's dale. And Melchizedek, king of Salem, brought forth bread and wine; and he was the priest of the Most High God. And he blessed him, and said, Blessed be Abram of the Most High God, possessor of heaven and earth. And blessed be the Most High God, which hath delivered thine enemies into thy hand. And he gave him tithes of all. And the king of Sodom said unto Abram, Give me the persons, and take the goods to thyself. And Abram said to the king of Sodom, I have lift up mine hand unto the LORD, the Most High God, the possessor of heaven and earth, that I will not take from a thread even to a shoelatchet, and that I will not take anything that is thine, lest thou shouldest say, I have made Abram rich; save only that which the young men have eaten, and the portion of the men which went with me, Aner, Eshcol, and Mamre; let them take their portion."

Now turn to Hebrews vii. 1-4, 21, where there is a divine comment on this passage from the Book of Genesis:

"For this Melchisedec, king of Salem, priest of

the Most High God, who met Abraham returning from the slaughter of the kings, and blessed him; to whom also Abraham gave a tenth part of all; first being by interpretation King of righteousness, and after that also King of Salem, which is, King of peace; without father, without mother, without descent" (that is, without genealogy), "having neither beginning of days nor end of life; but made like unto the Son of God, abideth a priest continually. Now consider how great this man was." That is what we are to do to-night—we are to consider how great the Lord Jesus Christ is, who is made "a Priest for ever after the order of Melchizedec."

"The Lord sware and will not repent, Thou art a Priest for ever after the order of Melchizedec."

Now, why does God swear? Surely His promise is enough for us. And so it is; but God in His infinite condescension to our weakness and our faithlessness has sworn in order that we may pay special attention to the things He has sworn to: and if you study carefully all the passages in the Old Testament where the figure of swearing is used of God, you will find that the swearing denotes that there can be no change of purpose with regard to them. For instance, what was the first thing that God swore to? He swore that the waters of Noah should never go over the earth again; so there can never be a flood over the whole earth again.

Then we read on the second occasion that God said to Abraham, "Take now thy son, thine only son Isaac, whom thou lovest, and get thee into the land of Moriah, and offer him there for a burnt-offering upon one of the mountains which I will tell thee of. And Abraham rose up early in the morning, and saddled his ass, and took two of his young men with him, and Isaac his son, and clave the wood for the burnt-offering, and rose up, and went unto the place of which God had told him." And there he did in intention what God had commanded him. And as he took the knife in his hand to slay his son, his own son, the son of promise, the Angel of Jehovah called out of heaven, and said, "By Myself have I sworn, saith Jehovah, for because thou hast done this thing, and hast not withheld thy son, thine only son, that in blessing I will bless thee, and in multiplying I will multiply thy seed as the stars of the heaven, and as the sand which is upon the sea shore; and thy seed shall possess the gate of his enemies: And in thy seed shall all the nations of the earth be blessed." So there you see God swore that through Abraham, and through his seed, the whole world must be blessed. The Church of God is being blessed by the knowledge of Christ at present, and when Israel receives the knowledge of Christ, then the whole world will be blessed through Israel.

Then on another occasion God swore to David: "I have made a covenant with My chosen, I have sworn unto David my servant, thy seed will I establish for ever, and build up thy throne to all generations." (Ps. lxxxix. 3, 4.) So that the throne of David must be once more set up. But I will not say anything about that to-night. Therefore, when God "swears," though all outward appearance may be against the fulfilment of the oath, the time will come when God's word will be fulfilled to the very letter, even though all the people and politicians in the world should try to prevent it.

Now, what has God sworn here? The person addressed is to be "a priest for ever after the order of Melchizedek," and David calls this person his Lord. (Ps. cx. 1.) "Jehovah." he says, "said unto my Lord, sit thou at My right hand, until I make thine enemies thy footstool." Now, David was King of

Israel at the time. There was no one in the land higher than he; therefore when he called that person Lord, the person must be some supernatural Being, and Jehovah says to this supernatural Being, "Sit Thou at My right hand, until I make Thine enemies Thy footstool." "Now, consider how great this man was."

How strangely Melchizedek meets us in the Book of Genesis! The first thing we are told is that his name was Melchizedek, or King of righteousness. So this King is a King of righteousness. "The sceptre of His kingdom is a right sceptre." (Ps. xlv. 6.) The great need of the world to-day is righteousness. Sin has made everything crooked, and what the world wants is men and women who can think rightly, deal rightly, and act rightly. Oh! that righteousness were more preached from the pulpits of all denominations! Now, the Lord Jesus is a King of Righteousness. When you come to Him He begins to set things *right*. Before you come to Him you are crooked; you are crooked to yourselves, crooked to God, and crooked to your neighbour; but when you come to deal with the true Melchizedek, then the desire for righteousness and justice comes to your soul. The first thing is that you should be right with God. The Lord Jesus Christ is King of Righteousness, because He sets the believer right with God first of all.

Then we read that He is King of Salem, which means peace. Some try for peace without righteousness, but cannot get it. There can be no peace in the heart, and there can be no peace in the world until righteousness is established. All the Peace Societies in the world will not bring peace to Europe until Jesus reigns in righteousness. And you never can have peace in your own soul until you accept the gift of righteousness from God, even that which is by faith of Jesus Christ; the same righteousness that Abraham had when he believed God. (See Phil. iii. 9, Rom. i. 17, iii. 21-26, iv. and v. 17-21.) God said to Abraham, "Look now toward heaven, and tell the stars, if thou be able to number them; and He said unto him, So shall thy seed be," though he had no child. "And Abraham believed in the LORD; and He counted it to him for righteousness." (Gen. xv. 5, 6.) Whenever a man becomes righteous with God he becomes righteous all round. "He that doeth righteousness is righteous, even as Christ is righteous." (1 John iii. 7.) So if there is a want of peace in your soul to-night, the reason is, perhaps, that you are not right with God and not right with your neighbour. *First*, King of Righteousness, and *then* King of Peace For instance, if I owe you a hundred pounds I do not like to meet you in the street; and if I do meet you I do not look you in the face. But when the account is settled I don't mind meeting you, and I can look you in the face. If any of you owe money to-night, go and pay your debts. Righteousness because Jesus is our King; Peace because Jesus rules within, and where Jesus reigns there is peace.

The next thing we notice about Melchizedek is that his genealogy is not recorded. Genesis is the book of genealogies. You read the genealogies of Noah, Seth, Abraham, and many more. You meet them on almost every page; but, strange to say, of this wonderful Being with whom we are confronted so suddenly we are told nothing about his father or mother, or pedigree, the beginning of his days or the end of his life. The writer of the Epistle to the Hebrews tells us this silence was designed. You know good music is known not merely by the music itself, but by the pauses in it. Sometimes in the middle of a piece there is a sudden pause, and the greatest musicians are known by their wonderful pauses. So if you want to understand that wonderful Book (holding up the Bible) you must know why God pauses sometimes. There is a deep reason for the silences of Scripture as well as for its words. We are told in the Epistle to the Hebrews the reason for this lack of genealogy, namely, He is "made like unto the Son of God, without beginning of days or end of life, therefore He abideth a Priest for ever."

Now we have come to the one important word —Priest. Yesterday we saw Him as a Prophet teaching us the truth. Now let us look in the face of Jesus to-night as a Priest. The prophets taught the people the truth about God. But it is not enough to know the truth about God; your soul needs communion with God. Now, God primarily designed that the whole nation of Israel should be a kingdom of priests. You read God's design for Israel in Ex. xix. When God redeemed Israel out of Egypt by the blood of the lamb, God said to Moses, verses 3 to 6:

"Thus shalt thou say to the house of Jacob, and tell the children of Israel: Ye have seen what I did unto the Egyptians, and how I bare you on eagles' wings, and brought you unto Myself. Now, therefore, if ye will obey My voice indeed, and keep My covenant, then ye shall be a peculiar treasure unto Me above all people, for all the earth is Mine. And ye shall be unto Me a kingdom of priests, and an holy nation. These are the words which thou shalt speak unto the children of Israel."

So God's original design for the nation of Israel was this: that it should be a holy nation, and that every man and woman in the nation should be a priest unto God; everyone a priest offering up spiritual sacrifices to God — a priestly nation. But Moses went up to the Mount to God, and while he was away the people hankered after externalism, and they said, "Up, make us gods, which shall go before us; for as for this Moses, the man that brought us up out of the land of Egypt, we wot not what is become of him." And they made the molten calf, and God was angry with them. and He sent Moses down from the mountain, and when he came down and saw what the people were doing, he was angry, and broke the tables of stone; and then he stood in the gate of the camp, and said, "Who is on the Lord's side? let him come unto me!" And the tribe of Levi joined him—Oh! that it were faithful always!—and that day they slew three thousand idolaters. (Ex. xxxii. 1, 26). And God said, 'I will choose Levi now to be My priest, and what the whole nation should have been, the tribe of Levi shall be.' Thus the tribe of Levi stood for the whole nation, and in the tribe of Levi He chose the family of Aaron. God's purpose for His redeemed people is the same now: that each one of them should be a holy priest to "offer the sacrifice of praise to God continually," "to offer up spiritual sacrifices, acceptable to God by Jesus Christ." (Heb. xiii. 15, 16, 1 Pet. ii. 5, 9.)

In this, as in everything else, Jesus Christ is the true *representative* Man: He is, what each one of us ought to be, a priest unto God (see Rev. i. 6); and His priesthood is perfect, because He is not only what we should be, but He gives us the power to be like Himself. "Consider how great this man was," greater than Abraham. Abraham was flushed with victory. He had with his three hundred servants defeated the kings of Shinar, Ellasar, and Elam, and Tidal king of nations, and he is returning from the battle when he is confronted by this strange being, Melchizedek; and Abraham falls down in worship before him, and instead of Melchizedek paying respect to Abraham, Abraham the conqueror pays respect to Melchizedek, and gives him the tenth part of the best of the spoils. And Melchizedek accepted it: and with high priestly dignity, blessed him whom God had blessed—him who had received the promises, him through whom the whole world was to be blessed —saying, "Blessed be Abram of the Most High God, possessor of heaven and earth." 'Thou art rich, thou art happy, Abram, for thou art a man of faith; thou art rich, for thou knowest God, and God possesses heaven and earth, and though thou dost not now possess a foot of the Land of Canaan, yet thou shalt possess it all! He who has Christ possesses all things. Oh! I am well off; every believer here is well off. I have great expectations; have you great expectations? Cheer up! If you are believers there is no need to be downcast, for you are well off; you possess God, the possessor of heaven and earth.

"A priest for ever," and hence a perfect one, for only that which is eternal can be perfect. The law cannot make anything perfect. All that the law can do is to show you your imperfection. The law is a looking-glass, and its object is to show you your need of cleansing. A looking-glass shows you your imperfections, unless you are too proud to see them. Many try to justify themselves before God, but when you look at the law you say, 'How ugly and filthy I am!' You would be a fool to try to wash your face with a looking-glass. The law does not cleanse from sin; therefore the law is imperfect, and the priesthood under the law is imperfect, for all that the legal priesthood can say is, 'You are wrong there and wrong everywhere.' They can only point out my imperfections, but they cannot take them away. That is all that the human priesthood does. But the priesthood of Jesus, the priesthood of Melchizedek, not only points out my sin, but says, 'Sinner, I take it all away from thee.' " For what the law could not do, in that it was weak through the flesh, God, sending His own Son in the likeness of sinful flesh, and for sin, condemned sin in the flesh"—that is, condemned it to death— "that the righteousness of the law might be fulfilled in us, who walk not after the flesh, but after the Spirit." (Rom. viii. 3, 4.) " The law made nothing perfect, but the bringing in of a better hope did, by the which we draw nigh unto God." (Heb. vii. 19.) The law keeps us at a distance from God. I am afraid of God because of the thunders and lightnings of Sinai. But Jesus bends down, and says, " Do not be afraid. Come unto Me all ye that labour and are heavy laden, and I will give you rest" (Matt. xi. 28). And then I draw near with boldness, through the blood of my High Priest; not through the blood of bulls and goats, but through the blood of Jesus, who offered Himself without spot to God (Heb. x. 19, 22, ix. 14). I draw nigh and offer myself to God, and my soul rejoices in the light of my Heavenly Father's countenance. This is what Jesus does, He takes the sinner by the hand and introduces him to the heart of God. His sacrifice is of eternal efficacy, and therefore perfect, and His cleansing is perfect, and He writes His law upon the heart.

The law of Moses was written on tables of stone, and was easily broken. But "I will make a new covenant with the house of Israel, and with the house of Judah ; not according to the covenant that I made with their fathers, in the day when I took them by the hand to lead them out of the land of Egypt; because they continued not in My covenant, and I regarded them not, saith the Lord. For this is the covenant that I will make with the house of Israel after those days, saith the Lord: I will put My laws into their mind, and write them in their hearts"—upon the "fleshy tables of the heart"- "and I will be to them a God, and they shall be to Me a people: . . . and their sins and their iniquities will I remember no more." (Heb. viii. 8, 9, 10, 12, with Jer. xxxi. 32, 33, and 2 Cor. iii. 3). That is the perfect law, under which we live now. God's Holy Spirit comes and dwells in your heart, and makes you love the things that God loves, and hate the things that God hates, making all things new. That is one reason why the law of Moses was powerless, because it could not give the Holy Spirit. But the law of Melchizedek not only tells us of the Holy Spirit, but gives Him to us, and He writes God's law upon our hearts.

Again, the Lord Jesus lives. He "is made, not after the law of a carnal commandment, but after the power of an endless life"; and by the Melchizedek priesthood He communicates the power of an endless life to all believers. That is what we need—the power to put this in practice; and Jesus says, "Because I live, ye shall live also." A priestly life ought to be a life of compassion for the ignorant and those that are out of the way. Jesus is a High Priest, Who can have compassion upon the people. A poor leper came to Him, saying, "If Thou wilt, Thou canst make me clean. And Jesus, moved with compassion, put forth His hand and touched him, and saith unto him, I will; be thou clean" (Mark i. 40, 41). Blind Bartimæus cried at the top of his voice, "Thou Son of David, have mercy on me!" "Hold thy peace," said the multitude. But he cried so much the more, "Thou Son of David, have mercy on me!" And Jesus, moved with compassion, touched his eyes, and immediately he received his sight (Mark x. 46-52). Then again there was a poor widow weeping behind her son's corpse; and Jesus was moved with compassion, and touched the bier, and said, "Young man, I say unto thee, Arise! And he that was dead sat up and began to speak. And He delivered him to his mother" (Luke vii. 11 to 16). Oh! what compassion there is in Christ! If there is anyone here with any sort of trouble in his heart, the Lord Jesus has compassion upon you; He is able to sympathise with you. We have not a High Priest who is not able to sympathise with our infirmities, but. "was in all points tempted like as we are, yet without sin." And He is not only able to sympathise with you, but He is able to succour you. "For in that He Himself hath suffered, being tempted, He is able to succour them that are tempted" (Heb. iv. 15, ii. 18).

There are those here to-night who know very well how the Lord Jesus has succoured them in the hour of temptation. Is not that the case, brother? Is not that the case, sister? I see by your faces that He has done so. He came in the day of your trial and degradation, and He came to succour you.

And, more than that, "He is able also to save them to the uttermost that come unto God by Him, seeing He ever liveth to make intercession for them." His life is a life of intercession. It is a grand thing to go to bed at night knowing that the greatest Being in the universe is praying for you and watching over you. "Peter, I have prayed for thee, that thy faith fail not; and when thou art converted, strengthen thy brethren" (Luke xxii. 32). "Father, I will that they also whom Thou hast given Me, be with Me where I am, that they may behold My glory, which Thou hast given Me; for Thou lovedst Me before the foundation of the world." (John xvii. 24). Is Christ praying for you? Christ prays for those who come unto God by Him. He is able to save to the uttermost—to the uttermost, completely, right through and through—from all dangers, from all difficulties, from all temptations. What has been your highest thought of salvation? Jesus will far exceed that. He will save you to the uttermost if you come to God by Him. If you come by your own righteousness, or by your own religious observances, you know nothing of that salvation; but if you come by Him He will save you to the uttermost. Oh! come by Him to-night!

Let me tell you one story about coming to God by Him. I have a great friend—Col. Oldham. We were in India together. He was telling me about his conversion. He said: "When I came out first as a lieutenant in the Engineers I went away from God. I gave up reading my Bible and praying, and some years afterwards I was known in the regiment as a confirmed unbeliever, an agnostic. I cast away all religion. But my heart was sad and dissatisfied. At last I came back to Scotland, and while there a friend of mine died. I had to go and sit in the house of death, because they were old family friends. Sunday afternoon came, and I was lonely. The church bell rang, and I thought, 'To pass the time I will go in; they say the man preaches well there.' As it happened, the good preacher was not there; a strange minister ascended the pulpit, and gave out his text—"Wherefore He is able also to save them to the uttermost that come unto God by Him, seeing He ever liveth to make intercession for them." I don't know what he preached about; I forget the sermon. But those words, "Save to the uttermost," rang in my heart, and I said, 'If I could only know that that is a reality; if I could only know that this Lord Jesus Christ does save people to the uttermost, then I would believe on Him; for nothing short of uttermost salvation will do for me. If I could be saved from unclean passions and unclean thoughts, and my heart made whiter than snow; if the promises in the Bible were made realities to me, *that* is the sort of Saviour I need.'" And he lifted up his heart to God that Sunday afternoon, and said, 'Lord, teach me what Thy salvation means. The words are grand words, and if there is reality in them teach Thou me.' And God taught him the reality of them, and in a short time he saw how the blood of Jesus cleanses the darkest stain away; how it satisfies all the claims of the broken law; how Jesus lives in His resurrection power to keep from sin within and sin around, that we may rejoice in God all the day long. Then Col. Oldham began to testify to those around him, and the fellows in the regiment saw the difference. That was many years ago, and he has been walking with God ever since.

So if you want salvation to-night you can have it by coming to God through Christ, Who is your true and everlasting Priest. No one can get on without a priest. The Lord offers you a Priest to-night—a Priest who can cleanse you perfectly, keep you perfectly, and present you in perfect glory when He shall have put all enemies under His feet, and when He shall take the kingdom and reign for ever and ever. Oh! it is worth your while, my brother, to know this great High Priest after the order of Melchizedek! Jesus Christ our Lord, Who has perfectly fulfilled all that was foreshadowed in the High-priestly work of Aaron and his descendants: having offered up the one perfect and sufficient sacrifice, oblation, and satisfaction for the sins of the whole world; and having entered for us, with His own blood, into the Holy Place not made with hands, "into heaven itself, now to appear in the presence of God for us." (Heb. ix.) And here, in the Most Holy Place, He exercises His office as the Great Melchizedek: ever interceding for us, ever blessing us, ever sustaining us with the Bread of Life, and with the Wine of the Kingdom, till He shall appear the second time to enrich with an eternal Benediction all who "walk in the steps of that faith of our father Abraham," all who "fight the good fight of faith," and who "lay hold on Eternal Life." (Rom. iv. 12; 1 Tim. vi. 12; 1 John v. 4, 5.) "This is the victory that overcometh the world, even our faith. Who is he that overcometh the world, but he that believeth that

JESUS IS THE SON OF GOD."

V.

The King of Glory.

Rejoice greatly, O daughter of Zion; shout, O daughter of Jerusalem; behold Thy King cometh unto thee; He is just, and having salvation; lowly, and riding upon an ass, and upon a colt the foal of an ass.

Zechariah ix. 9.

The kings of the earth set themselves, and the rulers take counsel together, against the LORD, and against His Anointed,
. . . .
Yet have I set My King upon My holy hill of Zion.

Psalm ii. 2, 6.

Our Lord Jesus Christ: . . . . the blessed and only Potentate, the King of kings, and Lord of lords;

1 Timothy vi. 14, 15.

The kingdoms of this world are become the kingdoms of our Lord, and of His Christ; and He shall reign for ever and ever.

Revelation xi. 15.

The King of Glory.

ET us read together the Revised Version of the Second Psalm, which is our subject for to-night:

"Why do the nations rage,
And the peoples imagine a vain thing?
The kings of the earth set themselves,
And the rulers take counsel together,
Against Jehovah, and against His Anointed, saying,
Let us break their bands asunder,
And cast away their cords from us.
He that sitteth in the heavens shall laugh:
The Lord shall have them in derision.
Then shall He speak unto them in His wrath,
And vex them in His sore displeasure:
Yet I have set My King
Upon My holy hill of Zion.
I will tell of the decree:
The LORD said unto Me, Thou art My Son;
This day have I begotten Thee.
Ask of Me, and I will give Thee the nations for Thine inheritance,
And the uttermost parts of the earth for Thy possession.
Thou shalt break them with a rod of iron;
Thou shalt dash them in pieces like a potter's vessel.
Now therefore be wise, O ye kings:
Be instructed, ye judges of the earth.
Serve the Lord with fear,
And rejoice with trembling.

Kiss the Son, lest He be angry, and ye perish in the way,
For His wrath will soon be kindled"
(Or, " when His wrath is kindled but a little)
" Blessed are all they that put their trust in Him."

The first six verses show the world in a terrible condition We see God the Father wondering at the state to which the world is come. The nations of the world, the rulers of the world, the judges of the world, the kings of the world, are taking counsel in their little brains; they are taking counsel against Jehovah, and against His Anointed. (Hebrew His Messiah.) They are trying to get rid of God's laws, of all that God has commanded, and by which He has bound us. " He that sitteth in the heavens shall laugh; the Lord shall have them in derision. Then shall He speak unto them in His wrath, and vex them in His sore displeasure. Yet I have set My King upon My holy hill of Zion." While man is saying. 'We will not have God's King,' God says, " Notwithstanding your rebellion, I have set My King upon My holy hill of Zion."

Then the Son of God is represented as saying: " I will declare the decree—God's decree—namely, Jehovah said unto Me, Thou art My Son, this day have I begotten Thee. Ask of Me, and I will give Thee those rebellious nations; those rebellious nations that lift up their hands against Us, and say, Let us break their bands asunder, and cast away their cords from us. I have given them to Thee, My Son; I have given them to Thee by Divine right; Thou art the only King reigning by right· Divine. And the uttermost parts of the earth for Thy possession. Thou shalt break them with a rod of iron; Thou shalt dash them in pieces like a potter's vessel."

Then the Holy Spirit begins to speak at the end of the Psalm. The Holy Ghost gives advice to the kings, to the judges of the earth, and every being in the world. Have you taken His advice?

"Be wise now, therefore, O ye kings; be instructed, ye judges of the earth. Serve Jehovah with fear, and rejoice with trembling; kiss the Son," *i.e.*, do homage, as in Gen. xli. 40, where Pharaoh said to Joseph, "Thou shalt be over my house, and according unto thy word shall all my people be ruled." In Hebrew it is "shall kiss thee," and it is translated in the margin of the R.V. "do homage."

"Blessed are all they that put their trust in Him."

That is the general meaning of the Psalm. Now I will confine myself to the sixth verse :

"Yet have I set My King upon My holy hill of Zion."

When God created Adam, He said to him: "Have dominion over the fish of the sea, and over the fowl of the air, and over every living thing that moveth upon the earth." (Gen. i. 28, 26.) God created man a king; God invested man with power; and for a short time the whole creation was obedient to Adam. But sin entered into the world, and erected its throne in Adam's heart, and man became disorganised through sin. When man gets disorganised within, he gets disorganised without too; and thus man lost his power to rule. Sin always destroys your power over yourself, and when you have no power over yourself you have no power over others. Peter the Great, of Russia, said one day, "I can govern my people, but who will teach me how to govern myself?" If Peter the Great had applied to the Lord Jesus Christ, He would have taught him to govern himself. What a man most needs is to have power to govern himself; but you can receive that only from God's King. So from Adam to Noah sin reigned, and man had no power to govern even himself.

Then the world got so bad, so full of sin and blasphemy, that God said, "I will destroy man, whom I have created, from the face of the earth; both man and beast, and the creeping thing, and the fowls of the air; for it repenteth Me that I have made them." (Gen. vi. 7.) And the flood came and destroyed all but the family of Noah. Then God chose the family of Abraham, and the kingdom of God was given to Abraham and his seed. Then we come down to David. And God found David a man after His own heart, and God sware to David: "Thine house and thy kingdom shall be made sure for ever before thee; thy throne shall be established for ever." (2 Sam. vii. 16, R.V.) And as God has sworn to this, nothing can disappoint the purpose of God.

Turn to Psalm lxxxix. 3, 4, R.V.: "I have made a covenant with My chosen, I have sworn unto David My servant: Thy seed will I establish for ever, and build up thy throne to all generations."

And again: "He shall cry unto Me, Thou art my Father, my God, and the Rock of my salvation. I also will make him My first-born, the highest of the kings of the earth. My mercy will I keep for him for evermore, and My covenant shall stand fast with him. His seed also will I make to endure for ever, and his throne as the days of heaven." (Verses 26 to 29.)

We see here that God has promised that the throne of David shall last as the days of heaven. "If his children forsake My law, and walk not in My judgments; if they break My statutes, and keep not My commandments; then will I visit their transgression with the rod, and their iniquity with stripes. But My mercy will I not utterly take from him, nor suffer My faithfulness to fail. My covenant will I not break, nor alter the thing that is gone out of My lips. Once have I sworn by My holiness; I will not lie unto David; His seed shall endure for ever, and his throne as the sun before Me." (Verses 30-36.)

This proves abundantly that God has bound Himself to establish David's throne, and that David shall never want a man to reign upon his throne. But David's seed committed iniquity, and apostatised from God, and became worse than the nations around them. God visited their sin with stripes. And the time came when King Nebuchadnezzar came to Judæa, and David's city was taken, and the seed royal carried captive to Babylon, and God handed over all power to the Gentiles. Thus the times of the Gentiles began B.C. 606.

Now, let us glance at Nebuchadnezzar's wonderful dream. (Dan. ii. 31.) "Thou, O king, sawest, and behold a great image. This great image, whose brightness was excellent, stood before thee, and the form thereof was terrible. This image's head was of fine gold, his breast and his arms of silver, his belly and his thighs of brass, his legs of iron, his feet part of iron and part of clay. Thou sawest till that a stone was cut out without hands, which smote the image upon his feet that were of iron and clay, and brake them to pieces. Then was the iron, the clay, the brass, the silver, and the gold, broken to pieces together, and became like the chaff of the summer threshing-floors; and the wind carried them away, that no place was found for them; and the stone that smote the image became a great mountain, and filled the whole earth."

This is the interpretation of the dream: "Thou, O king, art a king of kings; for the God of heaven hath given thee a kingdom, power, and strength, and glory. And wheresoever the children of men dwell, the beasts of the field, and the fowls of the heaven, hath He given into thine hand, and hath made thee ruler over them all. Thou art this head of gold."

So that the very power which God gave to Adam originally He now puts into the hands of Nebuchadnezzar. "And after thee shall arise another kingdom inferior to thee"—that was the Medo-Persian—"and another third kingdom of brass, which shall bear rule over all the earth." That was the kingdom of Greece under Alexander, and at his death it was divided amongst his four generals. And the fourth kingdom, (verse 40) which was the Roman," shall be strong as iron." Verse 44 : "And in the days of these kings shall the God of heaven set up a kingdom which shall never be destroyed; and the kingdom shall not be left to other people, but it shall break in pieces and consume all these kingdoms, and it shall stand for ever.'

In the days of the Roman Empire a little babe was born in Bethlehem of Judæa. Christ Jesus took flesh of the Virgin Mary, His mother, and in order to fulfil the words of the prophet Micah, He was born in Bethlehem. "But thou, Beth-lehem Ephratah, though thou be little among the thousands of Judah, yet out of thee shall He come forth unto Me that is to be ruler in Israel; whose goings forth have been from of old, from the days of eternity." (Mic. v. 2, marg.) And then the Lord Jesus lived those thirty-three and a half years of wondrous life, and at last the memorable day came when He rode into Jerusalem upon an ass, and offered Himself as King to the people of Israel, in order to fulfil the prophecy of Zechariah:—" Rejoice greatly, O daughter of Zion; shout, O daughter of Jerusalem; behold, thy King cometh unto thee; He is just, and having salvation; lowly, and riding upon an ass, and upon a colt the foal of an ass." (Zech. ix. 9.)

Jesus offered Himself as King, and the multitude rejoiced: they cut down palm branches and spread them in the way, and the disciples took off their garments and scattered them in the way, and shouted, "Blessed be the King that cometh in the name of the Lord; peace in heaven, and glory in the highest." (Luke xix. 38.) Then the King went into the temple, but He was rejected by the high priest and the elders and the scribes, and they sought to compass His death; and they succeeded. At last the King of Israel, with a cross upon His back, was led to Calvary They crucified the Lord of glory; "and the superscription of His accusation was written over His head in letters of Greek, and Latin, and Hebrew, THIS IS THE KING OF THE JEWS!" (xxiii. 38, with Mark xv. 26.) So Jesus was born King of the Jews, offered Himself to the nation as King of the Jews, was rejected as King of the Jews, and was crucified as King of the Jews.

Have you ever noticed what Jesus said to the multitudes who praised Him at the Mount of Olives? We read: "And when He was come near, He beheld the city, and wept over it, saying, If thou hadst known, even thou, at least in this thy day, the things which belong to thy peace!" (Luke xix. 41, 42.) That was the day on which Christ offered Himself as King to Israel; that was the day foretold by the prophet Daniel four hundred and eighty-three years before. (Daniel ix. 25.) That was sixty-nine "weeks" exactly, or four hundred and eighty-three years, "from the going forth of the commandment to restore and to build Jerusalem"; in the twentieth year of King Artaxerxes. Therefore Jesus said "in this thy day," for on that day the prophecy was fulfilled and the crisis of

Israel's history had come. But because He came in such a lowly and humble way they rejected Him. They said, 'Is He a King? He certainly speaks wonderful words, and does wonderful works; but is that lowly one the King of Israel?' And they rejected Him. And that is why Jesus is now rejected by the great ones of the earth; it is because He comes in lowly form at first. Truth always comes in lowly garb. Always beware of the man who uses long words, for you may be certain he does not know much truth. Truth is simple; it is clear. The lowly Jesus is rejected in London to-day because people want all their worldly pleasures, and amusements, and society. If Christ would allow them to have those things they would receive Him; but if Christ interferes with their family life, and their social life, and their church life—and He certainly will—'No,' they say, 'we will not have a King who is only riding on an ass. Give us a King caparisoned in worldly glory.'

Jesus rose from the dead on the third day. He rose as King triumphant over the grave, over sin, over temptation, over every sorrow that can beset us in our worldly pilgrimage. And forty days after that the King went back to His Father's right hand, and now He is hidden in the upper sanctuary. And because the King is hidden, the kingdom is hidden. But when He comes back again there will be a manifestation of the kingdom. Hence the whole dispensation of the Church is a "mystery"—*i.e.*, something hidden to others but revealed to the initiated. The kingdom is a mystery, and Jesus says, 'Unto you, My disciples, it is given to know the mystery of the kingdom of God; but to others it is not given. They will despise the kingdom, which is righteousness, and peace, and joy in the Holy Ghost.' (See Matt. xiii. 11 and Rom. xiv. 17).

Do you understand the "mystery" of the Parables in Matt. xiii.—the mystery of the kingdom of God? May I give you a running comment on Matt. xiii., that you may understand what is going on in the world now. Unless you understand this you will be deceived by events passing around us. At the end of the chapter Jesus said, "Have ye understood all these things?" The disciples answered, "Yea, Lord." Oh! that this may be true of us all!

The first parable of the kingdom is the parable of the sower. The sower goes forth, and the seed falls on four species of ground, and only that which fell upon good ground, which fell into a good heart, brings forth thirty-fold, sixty fold, a hundred-fold. This is the way the kingdom in mystery begins in your heart. You may go to church and hear a sermon, and a word drops into your heart; or a friend comes and asks, 'Are you saved?' And you are shocked; but the word falls into your heart. There is life in that seed-word. That is why the Bible makes such commotion in the world, because there is life in it.

What is the next parable? It is the parable of the tares. An enemy comes and sows tares. That is what happened soon after the Apostolic Age. The seed of God was sown pure in the first century, but from the second to the fourth century every single heresy and false doctrine that we see now was then sown. The enemy came and sowed tares.

After that comes the parable of the mustard seed. There you have the outward development of the kingdom of God. The growth of national churches, great organizations spreading their branches everywhere; but the fowls of the air came too, and lodged in the branches. The fowls of the air are a type of Satanic agency. The fowls of the air are said to have devoured the seeds that fell by the wayside.

"When anyone heareth the word of the kingdom, and understandeth it not, then cometh the wicked one, and catcheth away that which was sown in his heart." From the time of Constantine forward the Church entered upon a career of worldly glory—the fowls of the air lodged in the branches thereof.

The next parable—that of the leaven—denotes the inner working and development of evil in the Church. The leaven of false doctrine and evil living amongst the baptised members of the Church: for the leaven in Scripture seems always a type of evil; in fact, the Holy Ghost defines leaven as "malice and wickedness" in 1 Cor. v. 7, 8: "Purge out therefore the old leaven, that ye may be a new lump, as ye are unleavened. For even Christ our passover is sacrificed for us; therefore let us keep the feast, not with old leaven, neither with the leaven of malice and wickedness; but with the unleavened bread of sincerity and truth." There is much leaven in all churches, whether the Church of Rome, the Church of England, the Presbyterians, Methodists, Baptists, or Plymouth Brethren. Yet amongst all these Christ has His "little flock" of faithful disciples, and to these He refers in the following parables.

The parables of the treasure hidden in the field, and of the merchant seeking goodly pearls, show us the exceeding value of the Church to Christ, and the preciousness of Christ to the true members of His "mystical body." Christ gave all that He had for the sake of the treasure in the field, which is the world; and the true believer sells all that he has to obtain One Pearl of great price—even Jesus. These parables have a double fulfilment; for whatever is true of Christ is true of the believer in a lesser sense.

At last the mystery of God is finished; the net that has gathered of every kind is drawn to shore. They put "the good into vessels, but cast the bad away," and Jesus says, "So shall it be at the end of the world; the angels shall come forth and sever the wicked from among the just; and shall cast them into the furnace of fire: there shall be wailing and gnashing of teeth." The *mystsry* of the kingdom is over, and the *manifestation* of the kingdom begins.

But how will Jesus come? How will the manifestation take place? He will come *personally*. We read in Zech. xiv. 4. that "His feet shall stand in that day upon the Mount of Olives, which is before Jerusalem on the east; and the Mount of Olives shall cleave in the midst thereof toward the east and toward the west, and there shall be a very great valley: and half of the mountain shall remove toward the north, and half of it toward the south." That reminds us of what the angels said: "Ye men of Galilee, why stand ye gazing up into heaven? This same Jesus, which is taken up from you into heaven, shall so come in like manner as ye have seen Him go into heaven." (Acts. i. 11.) With the clouds of heaven He went away from Mount Olivet, and in the clouds He will come back to Mount Olivet, attended by myriads of angels.

And Jesus will come not only personally, but *visibly*. "Behold, He cometh with clouds; and every eye shall see Him, and they which pierced Him; and all the tribes of the earth shall mourn over Him." (Rev. i. 7, R.V.) He will come in the glory of the Father, and all His holy angels with Him. The angels sang His birth. When He was born at Bethlehem there was a multitude of the Heavenly Host praising God, and they will come again as His courtiers to bring Him down to earth.

The love of very many is now growing cold, and evil seems triumphant, and there are scoffers who say, "Where is the promise of His coming? For since the fathers fell asleep, all things continue as they were from the beginning of the creation." (2 Pet. iii. 4.) But Christ will come, and at a time when men are flattering themselves, and thinking that they have stamped out Christianity: therefore Christ says, "When the Son of Man cometh, shall He find faith on the earth?" (Luke xviii. 8.) The answer is, "No." For many shall apostatise from the faith, and the Church will forget the truth; more infidelity will be preached than faith, and spiritualism will be rampant; but "this gospel of the kingdom shall be preached in all the world for a witness unto all nations: and then shall the end come." (Matt. xxiv. 14.)

Now, the Spirit speaketh expressly that in the latter times some shall depart from the faith, giving heed to seducing spirits, and doctrines of devils; speaking lies in hypocrisy; having their conscience seared with a hot iron." (1 Tim. iv. 1, 2.) When Jesus comes "the trumpet shall sound, and the dead shall be raised incorruptible, and we shall be changed." (1 Cor. xv. 52.) "Then we which are alive and remain, shall be caught up together with them in the clouds, to meet the Lord in the air: and so shall we ever be with the Lord. Wherefore, comfort one another with these words." (1 Thess. iv. 17, 18.) After the Lord has gathered out of His kingdom all things that do offend, He shall set up His throne at Jerusalem, where is David's throne, and this jarring world will once more be ruled in righteousness, and enjoy peace.

Let me read you a description of what the world will be like under the Messianic and millennial reign of Jesus of Nazareth, the King of the Jews, from the Revised Version of Psalm lxxii.: "Give the King Thy judgments, O God, and Thy righteousness unto the King's Son. He shall judge Thy people with righteousness, and Thy poor with judgment. The mountains shall bring peace to the people, and the hills in righteousness. He shall judge the poor of the people, He shall save the children of the needy, and shall break in pieces the oppressor."

Notice how often the poor are mentioned in this Psalm. It is the problem of poverty that is setting politicians by the ears now; and Socialism and Communism are rampant, and will be more rampant still, according to Holy Scripture. Men try to live without God in society, and God is going to teach English society, and German society, and French society, and American society that they cannot do without Him, and that they cannot have peace without Him; so that all society will be convulsed by the lawlessness of the days before the Second Advent.

"They shall fear Thee while the sun endureth, and so long as the moon, throughout all generations. He shall come down like rain upon the mown grass: as showers that water the earth. In His days shall the righteous flourish; and abundance of peace, till the moon be no more. He shall have dominion also from sea to sea, and from the River unto the ends of the earth. They that dwell in the wilderness shall bow before Him; and His enemies shall lick the dust. The kings of Tarshish and of the isles shall bring presents: the kings of Sheba and Seba shall offer gifts. Yea, all kings shall fall down before Him: all nations shall serve Him. For He shall deliver the needy when he crieth; and the poor, that hath no helper. He shall have pity on the poor and needy, and the souls of the needy He shall save He shall redeem their soul from oppression and violence; and precious shall their blood be in His sight: and they shall live; and to Him shall be given of the gold of Sheba: and men shall pray for Him continually; they shall bless Him all the day long. There shall be abundance of corn in the earth upon the top of the mountains; the fruit thereof shall shake like Lebanon: and they of the city shall flourish like grass of the earth. His name shall endure for ever; His name shall be continued as long as the sun; and men shall be blessed in Him; all nations shall call Him happy. Blessed be the Lord God, the God of Israel, who only doeth wondrous things; and blessed be His glorious name for ever; and let the whole earth be filled with His glory. Amen. and Amen."

O God, hasten the kingdom of the Son of David, for His name's sake.

One word before I close. Are you a member of Christ's kingdom yet? Do you know how to enter the kingdom of God? "Except a man be born of water and of the Spirit he cannot enter into the kingdom of God." (John iii. 5.) "Verily I say unto you, Except ye be converted, and become as little children, ye shall not enter into the kingdom of heaven." (Matt. xviii. 3.) So I ask, dear souls, Are you all born again in this hall to-night? Have you received the blessing of the Holy Ghost through the seed of the Word? Has the Word of God borne fruit in your heart? Are you a member of Christ? "If any man be in Christ, he is a new creature: old things are passed away; behold, all things are become new." (2 Cor. v. 17). Has there been a time in your life when all things passed away, and when Jesus made all things new? Has He spoken peace to your soul? Is your heart at peace

because Jesus reigns? Surrender to Him to-night.
Enter His kingdom as a little child, and not as great
reasoners, and arguers, and theologians. Jesus wants
little children. Except you become as little children
you cannot enter the kingdom of Christ. O God,
bless anyone here to-night who is not yet a member
of Thy kingdom. If you do not become a member
of the kingdom of God in *mystery*; you cannot partake of the kingdom of God in *manifestation*. Oh!
we who are members of Christ, let us exalt our King;
let us rejoice, and manifest His grace, for the world
needs happy souls. The poor, sad world wants to
see some people who are happy and joyful.

O God, teach us how to show forth to the world
Thy power, and grace, and kingdom. May we
compel them to come in, that Christ may be glorified, and that they may sit down at the marriage
supper of the Lamb. For His name's sake. Amen.

  All hail the power of Jesus' Name!
   Let angels prostrate fall;
  Bring forth the royal diadem,
   And crown Him Lord of all.

  Crown Him, ye martyrs of your God,
   Who from His altar call;
  Extol the Stem of Jesse's rod,
   And crown Him Lord of all.

  Ye seed of Israel's chosen race,
   Ye ransomed of the fall,
  Hail Him Who saves you by His grace,
   And crown Him Lord of all.

  Hail Him, the Heir of David's line,
   Whom David " Lord " did call;
  The God Incarnate—Man Divine;
   And crown Him Lord of all.

Sinners, whose love can ne'er forge
  The wormwood and the gall,
Go spread your trophies at His feet,
  And crown Him Lord of all.

Let every kindred, every tribe,
  On this terrestrial ball,
To Him all majesty ascribe,
  And crown Him Lord of all.

Oh ! that with yonder sacred throng
  We at His feet may fall ;
Join in the everlasting song,
  And crown Him Lord of all !

VI.

What is His Son's Name?

The LORD hath said unto Me, Thou art My Son; this day have I begotten Thee.

Psalm ii. 7.

Who hath ascended up into heaven, or descended? who hath gathered the wind in His fists? who hath bound the waters in a garment? who hath established all the ends of the earth? what is His Name, and what is His Son's Name, if thou canst tell?

Every word of God is pure: He is a shield unto them that put their trust in Him.

Add thou not unto His words, lest He reprove thee, and thou be found a liar.

Proverbs xxx. 4, 5, 6.

God . . . . . Hath in these last days spoken unto us by His Son, whom He hath appointed heir of all things, by whom also He made the worlds;

Hebrews i. 1, 2.

What is His Son's Name?

OUR subject to-night is the Divinity of the Messiah of Israel, the Divinity of the Lord Jesus Christ. We have seen that He is a Prophet appointed by God to teach the truth ; that He is a Priest for ever after the order of Melchizedek, appointed by God to take away sin : and that He is God's appointed King upon the holy hill of Zion.

But, brethren, all these things would be nothing if He be not Divine ; and so to-night we have to consider this point : Is the Church of God right in worshipping the Lord Jesus Christ as God? The Unitarians tell us that we are wrong, and the Jews tell us we are idolators. When I got up this morning I spoke to the Lord Jesus, and He spoke to me. He has answered my prayers in thousands of instances. Am I an idolator? When Jesus stood before the high priest, the high priest "said unto Him, I adjure Thee by the living God that Thou tell us whether Thou be the Christ, the Son of God. Jesus saith unto him, I am ; and hereafter shall ye see the Son of man sitting on the right hand of power, and coming in the clouds of heaven." (Matt. xxvi. 63, 64 ; Mark xiv. 61, 62.)

He said He was the Son of God : is that a lie ? A great many people, Jews, Unitarians, Buddhists, will admit that Christ was a very good man, the best man the world has ever seen: but we cannot stop there. A good man speaks the truth. The Lord Jesus said again and again: 'I am the Son of God, and if you do not believe in Me, you will perish everlastingly.' Do you believe Him when He speaks in that way? You ask me: 'Why do you believe in the Divinity of Israel's Messiah?' I believe it because the Jewish Scriptures teach it. If I could not find it in the Old Testament I would not believe it, and if Christ was not Divine, then He was an impostor. If I did not believe in His Divinity I would throw away my Bible, and say: "Let us eat and drink, for to-morrow we die." (1 Cor. xv. 32.)

But as I know that Jesus is God, as I know He is the Son of God, and can give eternal life, and can change the heart within, and take away the love of the world, and save from the temptations of the world, the flesh, and the devil, and because I know He has made a radical change in my heart, and that no mere man can do that, I want to give you, Jews and Gentiles, some good reasons from the Old Testament why the true Messiah, the Lord Jesus, must be a divine Person.

Our foundation text says: "Who hath ascended up into heaven, or descended? Who hath gathered the wind in His fists? Who hath bound the waters in a garment? Who hath established all the ends of the earth? What is His Name, and what is His Son's Name, if thou canst tell?"

If we ask a Jew His Name, the Jew would at once bow reverently, and say: 'Adonai, the Lord, Jehovah.' But we go on and say: 'What is His Son's Name?' The Jew is silent. I have seen that happen more than once. The Jewish friend says: 'The Name of God is Jehovah, but it is blasphemy to say that God has a Son.' 'My brother,' we reply, 'this very Scripture attributes ascension to heaven, and descension, the gathering of the winds in His fists, the binding of the waters, and the creation of the world to God *and to His Son.*'

Then take another verse in Isa. vii. 14: "Behold the virgin shall conceive, and bear a son, and shall call His Name Immanuel," that is, God with us. But the Jewish friend might reply: 'Jesus was never called Immanuel.' 'His Name shall be called' is just the Hebrew way of saying: 'This shall be His character; He shall be God.' For instance, it says of Jerusalem, in the last verse of Ezekiel: "And the name of the city from that day shall be Jehovah-shammah : the Lord is there." That does not mean that the name Jerusalem will be taken away, but that during the millennial age the character of Jerusalem shall be changed, because of the presence of Jehovah in the midst.

Then in Isa. lxii. 4, we read: "Thou shalt no more be termed Forsaken: neither shall thy land any more be termed Desolate; but thou shalt be called Hephzi-bah, and thy land Beulah: for the Lord delighteth in thee, and thy land shall be married." That does not mean that the Land of Palestine shall be called Beulah, but that its character shall be changed. So when it says here that the virgin shall call His Name Immanuel, it means that His character shall be that of Immanuel, that is, God manifested in the flesh, God with us; and everyone into whose heart He has entered by faith knows that this is the truth. God is with us.

In Micah v. 2, we read: "But thou, Beth-lehem Ephratah, though thou be little among the thousands of Judah," (or, among the families of Judah) "yet out of thee shall He come forth unto Me that is to be Ruler in Israel; Whose goings forth have been from of old, from the days of eternity." That verse declares that some mighty Being shall be born in Bethlehem who has had a pre-existence from the days of eternity. The words can mean nothing else.

Now turn to Isa. ix. 6, 7 : " For unto us a Child is born, unto us a Son is given," and notice that it does not say the Son is born, and the Child is given ; He could not be a child before He was born : but He was the eternal Son of God before He was born into this world, therefore it says that " God so loved the world, that He gave His only begotten Son, that whosoever believeth in Him should not perish, but have everlasting life." (John iii. 16.) This is the character of that Child : " His Name shall be called Wonderful, Counsellor, the mighty God, the Father of Eternity, the Prince of Peace. Of the increase of His government and peace there shall be no end. upon the throne of David, and upon his kingdom, to order it, and to establish it with judgment and with justice, from henceforth even for ever. The zeal of Jehovah of hosts will perform this."

Then look at Ps. ii. 2. We find the kings of the earth gathering together against Jehovah and against His Messiah ; and He who is called " Messiah " in verse 2 is the " King " of verse 6, and is called " Son" in verses 7 and 12. " Jehovah said unto Me, Thou art My Son ; this day have I begotten Thee. . . . . Kiss the Son, lest He be angry, and ye perish from the way, when His wrath is kindled but a little." We are told to do homage to the Son, to give Him the kiss of allegiance, and the Psalm closes by telling us : " Blessed are all they that put their trust in Him." Now that must mean that He is more than man ; it must mean that He is a divine Being. A Jew is commanded to put his trust in no one but Jehovah, for we read in Jer. xvii. 5-8 : " Thus saith Jehovah ; Cursed be the man that trusteth in man, and maketh flesh his arm, and whose heart departeth from Jehovah. . . . Blessed is the man that trusteth in Jehovah, and whose hope Jehovah is: for he shall be as a tree planted by the waters, and that spreadeth out her roots by the river, and shall not see when heat cometh, but her leaf shall be green; and shall not be careful in the year of drought, neither shall cease from yielding fruit." If the Messiah of Israel be only a man, as the Jews of to-day tell us, then anyone who puts his trust in Him will be accursed, and perish from the way.

Again, there is a Being often mentioned in the Old Testament who is called The Angel of Jehovah. You know the word angel means messenger, one that is sent on an errand. God reveals Himself through this Being throughout the Scriptures; and this Angel of Jehovah, whoever He is, accepts all the attributes of Deity, and rebukes no one for worshipping Him, and calls Himself "Jehovah" again and again. I desire to show that this Angel of Jehovah is none other than "The Son given," Jesus, who was born at Bethlehem, died on Calvary, and rose again from the dead.

Let us begin with Gen. xvi. Hagar had fled from Sarai her mistress, and we read that "the Angel of Jehovah found her by a fountain of water in the wilderness. . . . And the Angel of Jehovah said unto her, I will multiply thy seed exceedingly, that it shall not be numbered for multitude. And the Angel of Jehovah said unto her, Behold, thou art with child, and shalt bear a son, and shalt call his name Ishmael; because the Lord hath heard thy affliction. And he will be a wild man; his hand will be against every man, and every man's hand against him; and he shall dwell in the presence of all his brethren. And she called the Name of Jehovah that spake unto her, Thou God seest me: for she said, Have I also here looked after Him that seeth me? Wherefore the well was called Beer-lahai-roi; behold, it is between

Kadesh and Bered." The meaning is: "The well of the living One Who seeth me." So there you have the Angel of Jehovah saying: "I will multiply thy seed exceedingly, that it shall not be numbered for multitude," and Hagar calls Him Jehovah.

Later on we read in chapter xviii. that Jehovah appeared unto Abraham in the plains of Mamre as he sat in the tent door in the heat of the day. As he looked up, three men appeared to him, and he bowed himself to the ground, and addressed one of these three, and said: "My Lord, if now I have found favour in thy sight, pass not away, I pray thee, from thy servant: let a little water, I pray you, be fetched, and wash your feet, and rest yourselves under the tree: and I will fetch a morsel of bread, and comfort ye your hearts; after that ye shall pass on: for therefore are ye come to your servant. And they said, So do, as thou hast said. . . . And they said unto him, Where is Sarah thy wife? And he said, Behold, in the tent. And he said, I will certainly return unto thee according to the time of life; and, lo, Sarah thy wife shall have a son. . . . And Jehovah said unto Abraham, Wherefore did Sarah laugh, saying, Shall I of a surety bear a child, which am old? Is anything too hard for Jehovah?" (It is the same word elsewhere translated "wonderful." "Is there anything too wonderful for Jehovah?") "At the time appointed I will return unto thee, according to the time of life, and Sarah shall have a son. . . . And the men rose from thence, and looked toward Sodom: and Abraham went with them to bring them on the way. And Jehovah said, Shall I hide from Abraham that thing which I do; seeing that Abraham shall surely become a great and mighty nation, and all the nations of the earth shall be blessed in him? . . . . And Jehovah said, Because the cry of Sodom and Gomorrah is great, and because their sin is very grievous; I will go down now, and see whether they have done altogether according to the cry of it, which is come unto Me; and if not, I will know."

Then the men left Abraham, "but Abraham stood yet before Jehovah. . . . . And Jehovah went His way, as soon as He had left communing with Abraham." So He Who is called man in verse 2, is called Jehovah throughout the rest of the chapter.

Now look at Gen. xxii. God had said to Abraham: "Take now thy son, thine only son Isaac, whom thou lovest, and get thee into the land of Moriah; and offer him there for a burnt-offering upon one of the mountains which I will tell thee of. . . . . And the Angel of Jehovah called unto him out of heaven, and said, Abraham, Abraham: and he said, Here am I. And He said, Lay not thine hand upon the lad, neither do thou anything unto him: for now I know that thou fearest God, seeing thou hast not withheld thy son, thine only son, from Me. . . . And the Angel of Jehovah called unto Abraham out of heaven the second time, and said, By Myself have I sworn, saith Jehovah, for because thou hast done this thing, and hast not withheld thy son, thine only son: that in blessing I will bless thee, and in multiplying I will multiply thy seed as the stars of the heaven, and as the sand which is upon the sea shore, and thy seed shall possess the gate of his enemies; and in thy seed shall all the nations of the earth be blessed; because thou hast obeyed My voice."

Notice here how the Angel of the LORD identifies Himself with Jehovah, and says: "I will bless thee. . . . . I will multiply thy seed."

IF YOU WANT TO BE BLESSED, *OBEY*.

Turn with me now to a most remarkable passage in Gen. xxxii. Jacob was in great trouble; he was afraid that his brother Esau would kill him; so he spent a night in prayer. "And there wrestled a Man with him until the breaking of the day. . . . And He said, Let me go, for the day breaketh And he said, I will not let Thee go, except Thou bless me. And He said unto him, What is thy name? And he said, Jacob," (that is, a supplanter). "And He said, Thy name shall be called no more Jacob, but Israel: for as a prince hast thou power with God and with men, and hast prevailed. And Jacob asked Him, and said, Tell me, I pray Thee, Thy name. And He said, Wherefore is it that thou dost ask after My name? And He blessed him there. And Jacob called the name of the place Peniel, for I have seen God face to face, and my life is preserved." Thus we find the Angel of Jehovah again identified with God.

Pass on to Ex. iii. Moses was keeping his father-in-law's flock, "And the Angel of Jehovah appeared unto him in a flame of fire, out of the midst of a bush: and he looked, and, behold, the bush burned with fire, and the bush was not consumed. . . . . And when Jehovah saw that he turned aside to see, God called unto him out of the midst of the bush." So you see the Angel of Jehovah was in the bush, Jehovah was in the bush, God was in the bush. And God said: "Draw not nigh hither: put off thy shoes from off thy feet, for the place whereon thou standest is holy ground." Holy ground because God was there, for nothing is holy unless God is there. If you want to know the secret of holiness, let God come into your heart. There is no holiness in the heart, or in the home, or in the Church, unless God is there. As soon as God went out of the bush, the bush was no more holy than any other bush.

"And Jehovah said, I have surely seen the affliction of My people which are in Egypt, and have heard their cry by reason of their taskmasters; for I know their sorrows; and I am come down to deliver them out of the hand of the Egyptians, and to bring them up out of that land unto a good land and a large, unto a land flowing with milk and honey; unto the place of the Canaanites, and the Hittites, and the Amorites, and the Perizzites, and the Hivites, and the Jebusites. .... And God said unto Moses, I AM THAT I AM: and He said, Thus shalt thou say unto the children of Israel, I AM hath sent me unto you."

Now turn to Judges vi. 11 : "And there came an Angel of Jehovah, and sat under an oak which was in Ophrah, that pertained unto Joash the Abi-ezrite: and his son Gideon threshed wheat by the wine-press, to hide it from the Midianites. And the Angel of Jehovah appeared unto him, and said unto him, Jehovah is with thee, thou mighty man of valour. And Gideon said unto Him, Oh my Lord, if Jehovah be with us, why then is all this befallen us? and where be all His miracles which our fathers told us of, saying, Did not the Lord bring us up from Egypt? but now Jehovah hath forsaken us, and delivered us into the hands of the Midianites."

If any of you are discouraged to-night because you think God is not blessing you, or because you think God has forsaken you, cheer up, my brothers; everything *seems* to be against you, but Jehovah has not forsaken you, and He will turn you into a mighty man of valour : for remember that the LORD cannot use you if you are discouraged with things around you, or things within you.

"And Jehovah looked upon him, and said, Go in this thy might, and thou shalt save Israel from the hand of the Midianites : have not I sent thee?" One look from God is enough to strengthen your heart.

Passing on to verse 19, we find Gideon presenting the Angel of Jehovah with the flesh of a kid and unleavened cakes : .... "And the Angel of Jehovah put forth the end of the staff that was in His hand, and touched the flesh and the unleavened cakes; and there rose up fire out of the rock, and consumed the flesh and the unleavened cakes. Then the Angel of Jehovah departed out of his sight. And . . . Gideon said, Alas, O Lord God! for because I have seen an Angel of Jehovah face to face. And Jehovah said unto him, Peace be unto thee; fear not: thou shalt not die. Then Gideon built an altar there unto Jehovah, and called it Jehovah-shalom."

Here again the Angel of Jehovah identifies Himself with Jehovah, and accepts the sacrifices.

In Judges xiii., where the Angel of Jehovah had told Manoah's wife that she should have a son; "Manoah intreated Jehovah, and said, O my Lord, let the man of God which Thou didst send come again unto us, and teach us what we shall do unto the child that shall be born. . . . . And the Angel of God came again . . . . and said unto Manoah, Of all that I said unto the woman let her beware. . . . . Manoah took a kid with a meat offering, and offered it upon a rock unto Jehovah: and the Angel did wondrously; and Manoah and his wife looked on. For it came to pass, when the flame went up toward heaven from off the altar, that the Angel of Jehovah ascended in the flame of the altar. And Manoah and his wife looked on it, and fell on their faces to the ground. But the Angel of Jehovah did no more appear to Manoah and to his wife. Then Manoah knew that He was an Angel of Jehovah. And Manoah said unto his wife, We shall surely die, because we have seen God. But his wife said unto him, If Jehovah were pleased to kill us, He would not have received a burnt offering and a meat offering at our hands, neither would He have shewed us all these things, nor would, as at this time, have told us such things as these."

"And the Angel did wondrously;" compare this with verse 17. "And Manoah said unto the Angel of Jehovah, What is Thy name, that when Thy sayings come to pass, we may do Thee honour? And the Angel of Jehovah said unto him, Why askest thou thus after My Name, seeing it is secret?" (or, "seeing it is wonderful," as in the R.V.) This links us to Isa. ix. 6, where the same word is used: "His Name shall be called Wonderful." Thus we are brought face to face with the Babe of Bethlehem, in the person of the Angel of Jehovah.

Dear friends, is the Lord "Wonderful" to you? Have you begun to believe in a Wonderful Saviour? for I find very few expect the Lord to do wonderful things for them in their families, in their business, in their churches, or in their personal experiences. He delights to do wonderful things. If the Gospels did not tell me anything wonderful about Jesus Christ I should not believe; but the first thing which meets us about the Messiah of Israel is that He is wonderful in His words, wonderful in His way, wonderful in His works, wonderful in His thoughts. "Never man spake like this Man," said the officers to the chief priests and Pharisees. (John vii. 46.) The Lord Jesus was "Wonderful," for He was born as the Son of God, and boldly proclaimed: "My Father worketh hitherto, and I work. Therefore the Jews sought the more to kill Him, because He not only had broken the Sabbath, but said also that God was His Father, making Himself equal with God. Then answered Jesus . . . He that honoureth not the Son, honoureth not the Father *which hath sent Him*," saying in effect, "I am the Angel of Jehovah, I am the Messenger of the Covenant." (Mal. iii. 1.) Take the Gospel of John, and study the passages in which Christ speaks of Himself as "sent of God," and then you will understand what is meant by the Angel of

Jehovah. "The Father sent the Son to be the Saviour of the world." "He whom God hath sent speaketh the words of God." "But I know Him: for I am from Him, and He hath sent Me." "And we know that the Son of God is come, and hath given us an understanding, that we may know Him that is true: and we are in Him that is true, even in His Son Jesus Christ. This is the true God, and eternal life." (1 John iv. 14; Jo. iii. 34; v. 17-19, 23; vii. 29; 1 John v. 20.)

Another of His names is "Counsellor." Are any of you in difficulties to-night, not knowing what to do next? You have come to a place where three or four ways meet: then go to the Wonderful Counsellor, and say: 'O Son of God, Thou manifestation of the Father's wisdom, give me counsel in this my perplexity; Speak to me; O Thou " in Whom are hid all the treasures of wisdom and knowledge."' (Col. ii. 3.)

Then He is "The Mighty God." The only other place in which that expression occurs is Isa. x. 21: "The remnant shall return, even the remnant of Jacob, unto The Mighty God." No Jew would dream of arguing that the mighty God does not here mean Jehovah, but in chapter ix. 6, because the passage gives countenance to the Messiahship of Jesus, they argue that it cannot mean Jehovah there, but some mighty General! Israel and Judah will never know what peace is, and their wanderings will not cease and the curse will not be removed until they return to The Mighty God; and when the heart of the Jewish remnant returns to God, then the veil will be taken away and they shall see God in the face of Jesus Christ. (2 Cor. iii. 14-18; iv. 6.)

This wonderful Being is also "The Father of Eternity." He who is, and was, and is to come. (Rev i. 8.) And "The Prince of Peace." He who has made peace through the blood of His cross for sinners : (Col. i. 20.) and will yet restore peace to this restless world.

And notice how all these characteristics are connected with the throne of David. "Of the increase of His government and peace there shall be no end, upon the throne of David, and upon his kingdom, to order it, and to establish it with judgment and with justice, from henceforth even for ever. The zeal of Jehovah of hosts will perform this."

We see plainly then—if words literally interpreted mean anything—that the Jewish Scriptures distinctly state that there is a Being upon Whom God the Father lavishes all His love, all His power, all His glory, all His excellence : that the heart of the Deity goes out to this wondrous Personage Who is called the Son of God, Who is the image of His Father's face, Who is the effulgence of the Father's glory, by Whom the Father created all things, and established the ends of the earth : and with Him He took counsel with regard to the creation of man, saying : " Let us make man in our image, after our likeness." From all eternity past the Son dwelt in the bosom of the Father. (Comp: Jo. i. 14, 18 ; Heb. i. 2, 3 ; Gen. i. 26 ; and Prov. viii. 22-31.) The Son was God's spoken Word to the world. We could not understand the inner thought of Deity but for the words spoken by God through Jesus. Jesus is the manifestation to us of God's mind. Some thoughts are passing in my brain, and they are expressed in words, and if I am an honest man, my words express my thoughts. And God has revealed the thoughts of His eternal mind to us by the Angel of Jehovah, Who was sent from God to men during the Old Testament dispensation ; and Who, in the fulness of time, was sent into the world, to be born of a pure virgin " made under the law, to redeem them that were under the law, that we might receive the adoption of sons." (Gal. iv. 4, 5.) And the time must come when God will give to Him the throne of His father David at Jerusalem, for that is the only place where David had a throne: and the promise made to David shall be literally fulfilled, and those who have denied it, shall be found liars in that day.

To each one of you I say: Add not to God's words nor take away from them, lest God take away thy name out of the Book of Life. And now " the Spirit and the bride say, Come. And let him that heareth say, Come. And let him that is athirst come. And whosoever will, let him take the water of life freely." It is Jesus, "the root and the offspring of David, and the bright and morning Star," Who has sent His angel to testify unto you these things in the churches. (Rev. xxii. 16-19.) Then come to the Son of God, for He is perfect and compassionate; He poured out His blood for us, and He gives eternal life through His sacrifice on Calvary. It was not the blood of man suffering for man; but God, in the infinitude of His love, has come down to us and taken our sins upon Himself. God, I may say, has done injustice to Himself, in order to suffer for us.

Ah! said the chief priests and the scribes, (Matt. xxvii. 40, 42; Mark xv. 31, 32.) "He saved others; Himself He cannot save. If Thou be the Son of God, come down from the cross. Let Christ the King of Israel descend now from the cross." These were cruel words, and yet they were true. "He saved others; Himself He cannot save." "For these things were done that the Scripture should be fulfilled." (John xix. 36.) Jesus the Son of God laid down His life for us miserable sinners: He was mocked by those whom He came to save: but He rose triumphant from the dead on the third day, instinct with life and power, and thus He was "declared to be the Son of God with power, ... by the resurrection from the dead:" (Rom. i. 4.)

So now if you want a true Saviour, an almighty Saviour, an everlasting Saviour, One that will endure when all others fail; Who will be faithful when all others are faithless, come to the Son of God. Kiss the Son, lest His wrath be kindled, and it may be kindled in a little time.

"BLESSED ARE ALL THEY THAT PUT THEIR TRUST IN HIM."

    The God of Abraham praise,
      Who reigns enthroned above;
    Ancient of everlasting days,
      And God of love!
    Jehovah, great I AM,
      By earth and heaven confessed;
    I bow and bless the sacred Name
      For ever blessed.

    The God of Abraham praise,
      At Whose supreme command
    From earth I rise and seek the joys
      At His right hand
    I all on earth forsake,
      Its wisdom, fame, and power;
    And Him my only portion make,
      My Shield and Tower.

    The God of Abraham praise,
      Whose all-sufficient grace
    Shall guide me all my happy days,
      In all His ways
    He calls a worm His friend,
      He calls Himself my God!
    And He shall save me to the end,
      Through Jesu's blood.

He by Himself hath sworn,
　I on His oath depend ;
I shall on eagles' wings upborne,
　To heaven ascend ;
I shall behold His face,
　I shall His power adore,
And sing the wonders of His grace
　For evermore !

VII.

The Passover Lamb.

Your lamb shall be without blemish, . . . and the whole assembly of the congregation of Israel shall kill it in the evening. And they shall take of the blood, and strike it on the two side posts, and on the upper door post of the houses, wherein they shall eat it. . . . . And the blood shall be to you for a token upon the houses where ye are, and when I see the blood I will pass over you, and the plague shall not be upon you to destroy you, when I smite the land of Egypt.

Exodus xii. 5, 6, 7, 13.

Christ our Passover is sacrificed for us: Therefore let us keep the feast, not with . . . the leaven of malice and wickedness; but with the unleavened bread of sincerity and truth.

1 Corinthians v. 8.

Ye were not redeemed with corruptible things, as silver and gold, . . . but with the precious blood of Christ, as of a lamb without blemish and without spot:

1 Peter i. 18, 19.

The Passover Lamb.

IN the name of God I invite you to a feast, dear friends. Some people, when asked to come to the Lord Jesus Christ, look as though they had received an invitation to a funeral! but I have never been commissioned by my Lord, Who is joy and peace, to invite you to a funeral. I invite you to contemplate the Lamb of God, and to take Him to yourself, with all the blessings He has bought for you by His precious blood; for "Christ our Passover is sacrificed for us: therefore let us keep the feast" (1 Cor. v. 7, 8,) therefore, dear friends, we are not going to speak of sentimental ideas, but of glorious realities: we want you to say from your hearts:

> Out of my bondage, sorrow, and night,
>   Jesus, I come! Jesus, I come!
> Into Thy freedom, gladness, and light.
>   Jesus, I come to Thee!
> Out of my sickness into Thy health,
> Out of my want and into Thy wealth,
> Out of my sin and into Thyself,
>   Jesus, I come to Thee!

Do not pass on these words to somebody else. We are often liberal in this respect, thinking in our hearts: 'That suits Mrs. So-and-So,' or 'My neighbour needs that.' Let us to-night apply them to ourselves.

> Out of unrest, and arrogant pride,
>   Jesus, I come! Jesus, I come!
> Into Thy blessed will to abide,
>   Jesus I come to Thee!
> Out of myself to dwell in Thy love,
> Out of despair into raptures above,
> Upward for aye on wings like a dove,
>   Jesus, I come to Thee!

Now the month in which the children of Israel were to kill the passover lamb was appointed by God to be the beginning of months to them. It had been the seventh month of their year, but God by the exercise of His own will appointed it to be the beginning of months. God must have had some good reason for changing the time-keeping of a whole nation; what then is the significance of this to us? The answer is that your life has not begun in God's sight until the cleansing blood of the Lamb is applied to your soul : you are a dead man before Him until you receive life by the blood of the Lamb of GOD. I would solemnly ask : How old are you? Have you yet had a *second* birthday? Several years ago, when working amongst soldiers in the south of Ireland, I asked a sergeant-major if he would kindly write his name in my birthday book, as I should like to pray for him at least once a year. He wrote : 'So-and-so, born July 27th, 1867.' 'Why,' I said, 'you are forty years old if a day : why do you put 1867?' His reply was : 'That is the date of my second birth. I do not like to think of the years gone before, because they were years of sin.' Now, not all Christians can give the exact date of their second birth as that sergeant-major did; but I am not particular as to the date of your birth, but I am very particular as to the fact, for "Except a man be born again, he cannot see the kingdom of God." (John iii. 3, 5.)

On passover night the whole Israelitish nation began a new life, a life of freedom. They were a nation of slaves until then, and the taskmasters' whip had come down upon their shoulders, and they cried, and hardly knew to whom they cried, but God heard their prayer, and said: "I am come down to deliver them out of the hand of the Egyptians, and to bring them up out of that land unto a good land and a large, unto a land flowing with milk and honey;" (Ex. iii. 8.) so they began a new life, a new national life, on Passover night. How very often in the Old Testament God dates events from the deliverance from the land of Egypt, as in 1 Kings vi. 1: "And it came to pass, in the four hundred and eightieth year after the children of Israel were come out of the land of Egypt, in the fourth year of Solomon's reign over Israel, in the month Zif, which is the second month, that he began to build the house of the LORD."

God has a chronology of His own: He dates from Redemption. Always remember that God reckons your life from your second birth, when you begin to live the Christian life, when you die to yourself, and to your learning and everything else, and you have the love and joy of Jesus in your soul. This month shall be to you, not to the surrounding nations, the beginning of months.

> Just as I am without one plea
> But that Thy blood was shed for me,
> And that Thou bidst me come to Thee,
> O Lamb of God, I come!

Notice the lamb was to be set apart on the tenth day of the month and to be slain on the fourteenth. There were four days in which the lamb was virtually slain, but it was not really slain until the fourteenth. Perhaps we have there a type of the four Dispensational Periods before the Coming of Christ: the Adamic Dispensation, and the Dispensations of Noah, of Abraham, and of Moses. And then comes the fifth, the Christian Dispensation. In the fulness of time

"God sent forth His Son, made of a woman, made under the law, to redeem them that were under the law, that we might receive the adoption of sons," just as the children of Israel became the sons of God on Passover night. "I brought you unto Myself," said God, (Ex. xix. 4.) and to Pharaoh the LORD said: (iv. 22, 23.) "Israel is My son, even My first-born: and I say unto thee, Let My son go, that he may serve Me: and if thou refuse to let him go, behold, I will slay thy son, even thy first-born." But Pharaoh would not obey; he had to yield however when once the blood had been sprinkled. And Satan cannot keep *you* in bondage if you claim your liberty through the precious blood of Christ with which you have been redeemed. (1 Pet. i. 18, 19.)

I want you to notice very particularly how the lamb was not to be eaten, and how it was to be eaten.

Have you found the secret of continuous communion with God? You know communion means fellowship, God sharing with you what He has, and you sharing with Him what you have: this is pictured for us in the eating of the lamb; for eating throughout the Bible is a symbol of fellowship, joy, sustenance and strength. So every true Christian, after the blood of the Lamb of GOD has been sprinkled upon him, learns to feed upon Christ in his heart by faith for the nourishment and delight of his soul.

There were three ways in which the lamb was *not* to be eaten: (1) It was not to be eaten raw: (2) nor sodden at all with water: (3) nor with any bread that was leavened.

What shall we learn from the first? Jesus says: (John vi. 63.) "It is the Spirit that quickeneth; the flesh profiteth nothing: the words that I speak unto you, they are spirit, and they are life." There is one thing that specially characterises the Christianity of the nineteenth century, which may be called eating the lamb raw. You may know a great deal about the geography and natural history of the Bible, you may be able to discuss points of doctrine, to give the pros and cons for various readings, you may be able to discuss the age and authenticity of the Books of Scripture; but all that is eating the lamb raw, and your soul is empty; your head may be stuffed with knowledge, but your heart is hungry, because you are not yet satisfied with *Christ*.

The second prohibition is: "nor sodden at all with water," *i.e.*, you are not to boil it down, and thus take all the strength out of it. That is what many people do to-day with the truth of the Gospel. They soften down the doctrines of Christianity to suit the popular taste. Some object to the Atonement, others to the future punishment of sin, others to the baptism of the Holy Ghost, therefore these subjects are barely alluded to. We are not to weaken the truth, so as to suit the present age, as is done, alas! in many religious periodicals of the day. God have mercy on the editors, and on the ministers who preach according to the spirit of the times, and not according to the Spirit of God! It is only when you speak what the Spirit of God tells you, that you act in accordance with the command 'Thou shalt not eat the lamb sodden at all with water.'

For an explanation of the third point let us turn again to 1 Cor. v. 7, 8. "Purge out therefore the old leaven . . . . the leaven of malice and wickedness." Now I am going to speak of a salvation worth having. "My soul doth magnify the Lord, and my spirit hath rejoiced in God my Saviour." The word translated "malice" denotes any evil habit that ensnares and degrades you; the word translated "wickedness" denotes the evil mind, the evil passion within you that prompts you to the evil habit. Purge out therefore the old leaven of evil habits and evil desires: all that debases, degrades, or defiles your humanity.

Some people say that these evil habits are to stay with us until we die! But God says: Purge them out: and if you can persuade yourself that this means they are to be with you all the days of your life, then I cannot answer for your moral sanity. "Purge out the old leaven," and let the stream of the blood of Jesus flow between you and evil passions and carnal desires; and let the Holy Ghost take possession of your heart, and He will cleanse in His own blessed way what you cannot cleanse. Is anything too hard for the Lord? No; not for the God I preach to you, Who is a wonderful Saviour. You can have no real communion with Christ so long as you play with any sin, nor can you have the power of the Holy Ghost.

"The blood of Jesus Christ, God's Son, cleanseth us from all sin." (1 John i. 7.) Praise be to God for His wonderful redemption. Praise be to God for a Saviour Who can deliver that young man who has tried to deliver himself, and has cried in the despair of his soul: 'O God, deliver me,' yet the deliverance has not come. Well, brother, trust the Lord Jesus now to purge your soul from leaven. "Search me, O God, and know my heart; try me, and know my thoughts; and see if there be any wicked way in me, and lead me in the way everlasting." (Ps. cxxxix. 23, 24; li. 10-13.) "Create in me a clean heart, O God;" (it must be a divine act of creation) "and renew a right spirit within me. Cast me not away from Thy presence; and take not Thy Holy Spirit from me. Restore unto me the joy of Thy salvation; and uphold me with Thy free Spirit: then will I teach transgressors Thy ways; and sinners shall be converted unto Thee." For sinners will then see that you have a Saviour worth having; and they will say:

'That is just what I need. If what that man says is true, that is just what will suit me.' And after having once trusted for this deliverance, keep trusting.

We now come to the way in which the lamb *was to be eaten*: and (1) it was to be "*Roast with fire*," which typifies both the suffering of Jesus, and the power of the Holy Ghost. You cannot separate the two, for it was "through the eternal Spirit" that Jesus "offered Himself without spot to God," that by His blood He might "purge your conscience from dead works to serve the living God." (Heb. ix. 14.) How different is the Bible when you open it under the teaching of the Holy Ghost from what it was before: how it sparkles when you open it solemnly and say: 'O God the Holy Ghost, teach me something about Jesus. O holy fire of God, burn Thy truth into my soul. Holy Spirit of God, make Thy Word "living, and powerful, and sharper than any two-edged sword" to me.' You will then eat the lamb roast with fire; everything about Jesus will become instinct with life and fire, for the Holy Ghost takes of the things of Christ and reveals them unto you. (See John xvi. 13-15.) You may read Commentaries all your life and not know Jesus. Beware of many of the books that are pouring out of the press in the present day. Make room for the Holy Ghost, the Giver of wisdom, and He will lead you into all the truth. Are you willing to be led? He will make you to lie down in green pastures, and lead you beside the still waters.

(2) The lamb was to be eaten *with the loins girded*. In 1 Pet. i. 13, we read: "Wherefore gird up the loins of your mind, be sober, and hope to the end for the grace that is to be brought unto you at the revelation of Jesus Christ." And in Eph. vi. 14: "Stand therefore having your loins girt about with truth," there are to be no loose garments about you,

but your mind is to be fixed upon Jesus. "My heart is fixed, O God, my heart is fixed; I will sing and give praise Awake up, my glory; awake psaltery and harp; I myself will awake early." (Ps. lvii. 7, 8.) When your heart is fixed, you begin to praise at once When your loins are girt about with truth, all your flabbiness and looseness of character is taken away.

(3) The children of Israel were to eat the roasted lamb *with shoes on their feet.*

Eph. vi. 15, tells us the spiritual meaning of this, "Your feet shod with the readiness of the Gospel of peace." Have you such shoes on? Readiness! Ready to do anything, ready to speak when God tells you, ready to do nothing when He tells you to be quiet. Oh! for ready and obedient souls! obedient in the underground railway, in the tram-car, in the public street, at afternoon tea; ready anywhere and everywhere. That is the sort of Christians we want; not church or chapel-goers merely, but Christians ready for service, Christians shod to serve God wherever they are. Then your witness will be simple and natural; your heart will not have to be a force-pump. God's love will flow in, and you will only have to let it flow out. That is having "your feet shod with the readiness of the gospel of peace."

(4) The passover must be eaten, said the LORD to Moses, with "*your staff in your hand.*"

There is the lamb upon the table, and the Hebrew father standing in the midst of his family, eating the lamb with one hand, and holding his staff in the other: his whole attitude showing that he is ready to depart, and is no longer *at home* in the land of Egypt, for the staff is the symbol of pilgrimage.

You who are born from above, and are already citizens of heaven, are to show to all men that you are "strangers and pilgrims on the earth." You are to confess that here you have no continuing city, but that you seek one to come. "For they that say such things declare plainly that they seek a country," literally "their native country." (See Heb. xi. 13-16; xiii. 14.)

True pilgrims do not carry much baggage, nor need a grand home down here, nor will they burden themselves with the good things of Egypt: for "they desire a better country, that is an heavenly: wherefore God is not ashamed to be called their God: for He hath prepared for them a city."

(5) The redeemed people were to eat the lamb *in haste.*

There was to be no lingering behind in Egypt, for Egypt was doomed. "Remember Lot's wife." She was led out of Sodom by the angel's hand, but she longed after Sodom in her heart, and so the judgment of God fell upon her. Many in this age have come out of the world professedly, but their hearts are still in the world's society and amusements. "Remember Lot's wife." It is a dangerous thing to make a false profession to the Holy Ghost. Away, away from the doomed city, to my native country, in the company of my Lord Jesus. Make a clean cut with the world to-night, and let it be known; and you will suffer persecution. "Blessed are ye, when men shall revile you, and persecute you, and shall say all manner of evil against you falsely, for My sake. Rejoice, and be exceeding glad: for great is your reward in heaven: for so persecuted they the prophets which were before you." (Matt. v. 11, 12.)

(6) Our Passover feast is to be eaten "*with the unleavened bread*" of sincerity and truth. (See 1 Cor. v. 8, and pages 119 and 120.)

If anything goes wrong in your Christian life, don't deny it, but confess it, and put it away. Say: 'Lord, I have done wrong; I have taught wrongly. Lord, make me clean.' Be true, and transparent, walking in the light—" sincere and without offence till the day of Christ." (Phil. i. 10.)

(7) The lamb must be eaten "*with bitter herbs*," which reminds us of the words of the Lord Jesus: (John xvi. 33.) "In the world ye shall have tribulation :" but, praise God, there will be no bitter herbs in the glory above. There will always be some tears here until Christ comes and wipes them all away: *then* "there shall be no more death, neither sorrow, nor crying, neither shall there be any more pain: for the former things are passed away." (Rev. xxi. 4.) Then we shall appear at the Marriage Supper of the Lamb, and enter for ever into the joy of our Lord.

What shall we learn concerning the three parts of the lamb which were to be eaten, "His head, with his legs, and with the purtenance thereof"?

"The head" of the Lamb of God denotes the thoughts, the words, the truths, that came out of His mighty mind: and "the legs" denote the walk of Christ, the conduct of Christ in the world. Whenever you take in the truth of Christ you are to turn it into practice. They shall eat his head *with* his legs. One great evil of to-day is that so many eat the head without the legs: admiring Jesus as a Teacher, but not turning the truth He taught into practice. "If we say that we have fellowship with Him, and walk in darkness, we lie, and do not the truth: But if we walk in the light, as He is in the light, we have fellowship one with another, and the blood of Jesus Christ His Son cleanseth us from all sin." (1 John i. 6, 7.) "He that saith he abideth in Him, ought himself also so to walk, even as He walked." (1 John ii. 6.) O God, teach us to walk like Jesus; teach us to *do* the truth Jesus did ; not only to take Thy holy words into our heads; but to let them move our feet, and rule our lives.

"And with the purtenance thereof," or "with the the inwards thereof" as in the Revised Version.

That is, the heart of the lamb is to be taken into yourself. The heart of the Lamb! You are to feast upon the affections, the love of Jesus in your inmost soul. If there is any lonely pilgrim longing for love to-night, thy God makes thee a present of the heart of His Son: oh! may He teach thee to abide in the love of Christ. "Abide in My love. If ye keep My commandments, ye shall abide in My love; even as I have kept My Father's commandments, and abide in His love." (John xv. 9, 10.)

A few words to those who want to be saved from the wrath to come. God says: "And ye shall take a bunch of hyssop, and dip it in the blood that is in the basin, and strike the lintel and the two side posts with the blood that is in the basin: and none of you shall go out at the door of his house until the morning. For the Lord will pass through to smite the Egyptians; and when He seeth the blood upon the lintel, and on the two side posts, the Lord will pass over the door, and will not suffer the destroyer to come in unto your houses to smite you."

Hyssop denotes faith, for in Heb. xi. 28, it is written: "Through faith Moses kept the passover, and the sprinkling of the blood." In reality it was by means of hyssop. God did not appoint a very rare plant by which to sprinkle the blood. No; that would be giving salvation with one hand and taking it away with the other; but the plant He appointed was very common in the East, and most easily obtained.

The same faith that you put in father or mother, or brother or sister, or friend, you are to put in God your Saviour. When your father says: 'My son, I will give you such and such a thing to-morrow,' you believe him, for he is your father: and when God says: "My child, I give you eternal life through My Son," you must believe Him. You have not got to work up faith. Faith is not a rare exotic plant only found in spiritual hot-houses. The faith that saves the soul; the faith that brings forgiveness, that cleanses the inner man; the faith that brings God's divine creation into the heart—that faith is simply resting on Jesus like a little child on its mother's bosom, apart from any feeling whatever. Whether you are feeling happy or miserable, cheerful or downcast, just come and rest upon the word and testimony of your Saviour. Believe that the Lord Jesus Christ died for you, that He has taken away your sins, that He has linked you to Himself, and thank Him. The least you can do is to thank Him. The word of Jesus makes your soul *sure*; the blood of Jesus makes your soul *safe*. The blood was sprinkled upon the two side posts in order to save from danger on the right hand and on the left: the blood was sprinkled on the lintel, to save from the wrath of God coming down from above. Will you not take your bunch of hyssop and say to the death-angel: 'Thou canst not touch me, pass on, for I am safe under the blood-stained lintel: Jesus is my perfect Saviour from sin within and around.' "Being now justified by His blood, we shall be saved from wrath through Him." (Rom. v. 9.)

The sprinkled blood is the *one thing God looks for:* He saw no blood on Pharaoh's palace, and the destroyer went in unhindered. Does He see the blood of Jesus Christ His Son sprinkled upon you? Whatever you do, do not trample upon that "precious blood": for notice in Ex. xii. that no blood was ordered to be sprinkled on the floor of the threshold, lest it should be trodden under foot. With all reverence and with sorrow of soul I would say that if anyone rejects the full salvation which Christ Jesus has purchased for them with His own blood, he is trampling under foot the Son of God, and counting the blood of the covenant an unholy thing, and doing despite to the Spirit of grace. (Heb. x. 29.) May God save you from such a sin, and enable you to say with all your heart in simple faith :

> Out of my shameful failure and loss,
>   Jesus, I come ! Jesus, I come !
> Into the glorious gain of Thy cross,
>   Jesus, I come to Thee !
> Out of earth's sorrows into Thy balm,
> Out of earth's storms and into Thy calm,
> Out of distress to jubilant psalm,
>   Jesus, I come to Thee !

www.ingramcontent.com/pod-product-compliance
Lightning Source LLC
Chambersburg PA
CBHW022140160426
43197CB00009B/1374